Freemasonry in Old Buffalo

Dedicated to Terrence M. Connors,
a distinguished Buffalonian
and outstanding attorney

Freemasonry in Old Buffalo

James Leroy Nixon's
History of Buffalo Consistory

Introduced and Edited by
Paul Rich

WESTPHALIA PRESS
An imprint of Policy Studies Organization

Freemasonry in Old Buffalo
James Leroy Nixon's *History of Buffalo Consistory*

All Rights Reserved © 2013 by Policy Studies Organization

Westphalia Press
An imprint of Policy Studies Organization
dgutierrezs@ipsonet.org

All rights reserved. No part of this book may be reproduced or transmitted in any form or by any means graphic, electronic, or mechanical, including photocopying, recording, taping, or by any information storage or retrieval system, without the permission in writing from the publisher.

For information:
Westphalia Press
1527 New Hampshire Ave., N.W.
Washington, D.C. 20036

ISBN-13: 978-1-935907-03-9
ISBN-10: 1935907034

Updated material and comments on this edition can be found at the Policy Studies Organization website:
http://www.ipsonet.org/

FREEMASONRY IN OLD BUFFALO: INTRODUCTION TO NEW EDITION

SCARCE old books full of names are ambrosia for genealogists, and James Leroy Nixon's account of the Buffalo Consistory certainly mentions an army of Victorian and Edwardian Buffalo worthies. The volume is also notable for recording the expansion of the Scottish Rite of Freemasonry in upstate New York. As Nixon explains, this is a set of degrees, which requires the candidate to already have become a Mason by taking the first three degrees. Sometimes the degrees are described as higher degrees, but members prefer to say more modestly that they are improving their knowledge and that the Scottish Rite is a sort of Masonic university.

The degrees are actually plays in which the initiate acts a central role. Each of these plays expands on the moral and ethical teachings of the initial three Masonic degrees. There are four separate bodies that supervise the giving of the Scottish Rite degrees. The fourth through the fourteen degrees are given in a Lodge of Perfection. The fifteenth and sixteenth degrees are given by a Council of the princes of Jerusalem. The seventeenth and eighteenth degrees are conferred by a Chapter of Rose Croix. The nineteenth through the third-second degrees are the responsibility of the

Consistory, which also has some oversight over the entire process. The thirty-third degree is given by the Supreme Council.

The degrees in Buffalo follow the writ of the Northern Jurisdiction of the Scottish Rite and differ from those given in some states by the Southern Jurisdiction. This is the order for initiations in Buffalo:

      Lodge of Perfection – 4° – 14° Degrees

4° – Secret Master
5° – Perfect Master
6° – Intimate Secretary
7° – Provost and Judge
8° – Intendant of the Building
9° – Master Elect of the Nine – North
10° – Master Elect of the Fifteen – North
11° – Sublime Master Elected – North
12° – Grand Master Architect
13°- Master of the Ninth Arch
14° – Grand Elect Mason
      Council of Princes of Jerusalem – 15° – 16° Degrees
15° – Knight of the East or Sword
16° – Prince of Jerusalem
      Rose Croix – 17° – 18° Degrees
17°- Knight of the East and West
18°- Knight of the Rose Croix
      Consistory – 19° – 32° Degrees
19° – Grand Pontiff
20° – Master ad Vitam
21° – Patriarch Noachite
22° – Prince of Libanus

23° – Chief of the Tabernacle
24° – Prince of the Tabernacle
25° – Knight of the Brazen Serpent
26° – Prince of Mercy
27° – Commander of the Temple
28° – Knight of the Sun
29° – Knight of St. Andrew
30° – Grand Inspector
31° – Knight Aspirant
32° – Sublime Prince of the Royal Secret
33° – Sovereign Grand Inspector General

The Buffalo Consistory long ago left its Delaware Avenue location and now has a building on Union Road in Cheektowaga. But the notable Buffalonians mentioned in this volume would have no difficulty in recognizing the ceremonies. Nor will genealogists lack for information about their fraternalist ancestors.

Paul Rich

BUFFALO CONSISTORY HOUSE AND CATHEDRAL IN DELAWARE AVENUE

HISTORY OF
BUFFALO CONSISTORY
A. A. S. R.

AND CO-ORDINATE BODIES FROM THE INSTITUTION OF PALMONI LODGE OF PERFECTION IN 1867, TO THE CLOSE OF 1915

By JAMES LEROY NIXON, 32°
Sovereign Prince of Palmoni Council
Princes of Jerusalem

ORIENT OF BUFFALO
December 31
1915

JAMES L. NIXON, 32°
AUTHOR AND COMPILER OF THIS HISTORY, AND SOVEREIGN PRINCE OF
PALMONI COUNCIL, PRINCES OF JERUSALEM

DEDICATION

❖ ❖

To the Sovereign Grand Commander of the Supreme Council Sovereign Grand Inspectors General, of the Ancient Accepted Scottish Rite for the Northern Jurisdiction of the United States of America, Most Puissant Barton Smith, 33°, of Toledo, O.; Illustrious William Homan, 33°, Active, Deputy for New York State of the Supreme Council; Illustrious George K. Staples, 33°, Commander-in-Chief of Buffalo Consistory; to the Officers and Members of the Co-ordinate Bodies, whose loyalty and zeal have been most potent factors in the successful promulgation of the Rite in the Valley of Buffalo, and to the memory of those earlier Brothers, who, in Patience and Humility laid the foundation of our imposing Masonic edifice, this book is affectionately

Dedicated

by

The Author

"AB INITIO"

First was the seed, planted and nourished well
    By the immortal twenty-one,
To spring a tender shoot, of doubtful growth,
    Beset by adverse winds, its sun
Darkened by clouds of a disturbing doubt;
    Threatened by many hostile hands
But struggling bravely on to gain, at last,
    Release from its restraining bands.

Fires scourged, but still refinement brought,
    Leaving pure gold in lieu of dross,
And as the years of trial passed, the shrub
    Became a spreading tree, to toss
Its pliant branches high o'er Orient lands,
    To yield its harvest rich of golden fruit,
The fruit of a devout and true Fraternity,
    Into a thousand waiting, eager hands.

Today, it stands a giant in its strength,
    Unscathed by storm, or vandal hands,
Symmetrical and sturdy as the oak,
    A landmark for the craft of many lands;
Its verdant leaves a canopy, to shield
    An army from the slings of hate;
Its trunk a pillar, imperishable as truth,
    Which naught of calumny can ere abate.

                                J. L. N.

INTRODUCTION

BUFFALO Consistory, in its conception and in its completion, is a striking example of what can be accomplished by men banded together by the ties of a true fraternity under the influence of Brotherly Love. As they stand today, the Scottish Rite Bodies of the Valley of Buffalo represent so much of devotion to an ideal; loyalty to principle and consistent exemplification of Fraternal Brotherhood, as to make them a model after which others well might pattern. In the following pages the author has sought to place upon permanent record the principal events in the life of Buffalo Consistory, without embelishment of flowery expression, or classic phrase. He has aimed to give to the reader, especially to members of the Rite, a clear conception of the obstacles overcome, the struggles endured, the loyalty demanded and received, the effort required to bring Buffalo Scottish Rite bodies up to their present high plane of excellence and effectiveness. Accuracy of dates and correctness of incident have been his constant aim. Completeness and comprehensiveness have been sought. And with all, there has been a desire and an effort, to make clear the underlying principles of the great organization of which Buffalo Consistory is an integer; to impress upon the brother, as yet outside the charmed circle, the advantages presented and the benefits to be derived from affiliation with that band of devoted workers, who call Consistory House their "Home." In all it has been a labor of love, both for the great Fraternity, and for those fellow craftsmen who have wrought patiently and well in the upbuilding of our substantial Scottish Rite edifice. Thanks and appreciation are due and hereby extended to Secretary Harry D. Hosmer, to Ill. Charles W. Mann and to all others who, by suggestion or assistance, have aided in the preparation of this book, which now goes to the consideration, and I trust approval, of the Brethren.

                JAMES LEROY NIXON, 32°.

Buffalo, N. Y.,
December 31, 1915.

ORIGIN AND DEVELOPMENT OF SCOTTISH RITE MASONRY

Brief Sketch of the Order, from the Beginning, About 1717, Until the Organization of Palmoni Lodge of Perfection.

IN attempting to chronicle the history of Buffalo Consistory and its co-ordinate bodies, it is eminently fitting that there should be given, in connection therewith, a brief sketch of the Ancient Accepted Scottish Rite, of which the Buffalo Body forms an integral part. From the most reliable of Masonic historical sources, we learn that following the dispersion of the Templars, culminating with the burning to death in Paris on March 11, 1314, of the Grand Master of Masons, Jacques de Molay, and the scattering of members of the order to various countries to escape the vindictiveness of the French King, Philip the Fair, there was for a long period, little activity in the Craft. Hostility of the Jesuits had been pronounced and as the educational advantages of the period were only enjoyed by the priesthood, the nobility retrograded and little attention was given to those principles of development which had actuated the Masonic leaders. After the invention of the art of printing, learning became gradually more popular, but it was not until what is known as the "revival of 1717," that Masonic activity became marked. One writer tells us that during the middle portion of the 18th century, "the invention of new degrees was continuous, but most of them soon passed into oblivion."

Selecting The Degrees.

Of course the three degrees of Entered Apprentice, Fellow Craft and Master Mason, were the source from whence this prolific development of degrees sprang, and these three degrees with twenty-two others, were selected to compose a Rite which was destined to retain its vitality and to spread its influence throughout the world. This Rite was known as the "Ancient and Accepted Rite."

There has been much speculation as to the manner in which these degrees were selected and arranged, but Ill. Brother Albert Gallatin Mackey, M. D., in his "History of Freemasonry," gives the following as what he considers the most reasonable statement: He says:

Carried To Berlin.

"The Chevalier de Bonneville established a Chapter of twenty-five degrees of the so-called 'High Degrees,' in Paris, in 1754. The adherents and followers of the House of the Stuarts had made the College of Clermont their asylum, they being mostly Scotchmen. One of these degrees was the Scottish Master. The new Body organized in Charleston, South Carolina, in 1801

MOST PUISSANT BARTON SMITH, 33°
SOVEREIGN GRAND COMMANDER OF THE SUPREME COUNCIL, SOVEREIGN
GRAND INSPECTORS GENERAL OF THE ANCIENT ACCEPTED
SCOTTISH RITE, FOR THE NORTHERN JURISDICTION
OF THE UNITED STATES OF AMERICA

and gave the name of 'Scottish Rite' to these degrees, which name ever since that time has characterized the Rite all over the world. So it will be observed that the present title of the Rite is really an Americanism after all. The name previously given to these degrees was the "Rite of Perfection."

"The Marquis de Lernais carried these degrees to Berlin in 1758 and they were introduced into and adopted by the Grand Lodge. The Rite was revived in Paris in the same year. But in consequence of the interference of the Jesuits, who, finding that their former efforts had not succeeded in finally suppressing the Rite, 'sowed seeds of dissension' and a new organization was formed, called the 'Council of the Knights of the East.' In 1771, however, both organizations became incorporated with the Grand Orient of France, which held the Rite of Perfection within itself."

What is known as Scottish Rite Masonry was active long before its introduction in America, for it is asserted that in 1762, Frederick the Great, who had taken under his patronage all of Masonry in Germany, formed and promulgated what has been known ever since then as the Grand Constitutions of 1762.

IMPROVED BY FREDERICK.

"The 'Rite of Perfection' which for a quarter of a century, with many struggles, had not fully accomplished the work proposed for it by its authors, was improved, it is said, by Frederick himself, by a reorganization and reconstruction which placed it on a higher standard in its philosophy and its teachings; eight other degrees were added to it and the name was changed to 'The Ancient and Accepted Scottish Rite of Freemasonry.' The Grand Constitutions of 1786 were ratified and signed by Frederick in Berlin, in May of that year. By these constitutions of 1786, Frederick the Great resigned the authority he had held from 1762, as Grand Commander of Princes of the Royal Secret and Supreme Chief of the Scottish Rite, or of Perfection. His Masonic prerogatives were by the same document deposited with a council for each nation, to be composed of Sovereign Grand Inspectors General of the Thirty-third and last degree of legitimate Freemasonry, limited in numbers to that of the years of Christ on earth. The Grand Constitutions formed in 1762 were ratified in Bordeaux, October 25th, of that year, and were proclaimed as the governing laws for all the several bodies of the 'Rite of Perfection,' over the two hemispheres.''

Prior to this, Stephen Morin was invested with power, by the Grand Consistory of Sublime Princes of the Royal Secret, in Paris, on the 27th of August, 1761, to carry the Rite of Perfection to America. He received a Patent as his credential. Morin landed at Kingston, Jamaica, before reaching America, where he appointed Henry Francken a Deputy Inspector-General. Other deputies were named by him, all of whom were supplied with copies of the Grand Constitutions adopted in 1762.

Francken visited the North American colonies, where he gave an appointment to Moses M. Hayes at Boston, Mass. Francken also established a Lodge at Albany, N. Y. This was a Lodge of Perfection of the 14th degree, and is believed to have been the first body of the "Rite of Perfection," planted on the continent of North America. This was presumably in 1767.

Again referring to the history written by Ill. Brother Mackey, we find that "Brother DaCosta was made Deputy Inspector General of South Carolina by Hayes, in 1781; he also appointed Solomon Bush Deputy for Pennsylvania and B. M. Spitzer Deputy for Georgia. DaCosta established in Charleston, in 1783, a 'Sublime Grand Lodge of Perfection.'"

Princes Of Jerusalem.

A Council of Princes of Jerusalem was duly constituted in Charleston, and Meyers, Spitzer and Frost were present and installed the officers on February 20, 1788. A Council of Knight Kadosh was organized in Philadelphia in 1796, by refugees from San Domingo. In New York City a Chapter of Rose Croix, 18th degree, was established in 1797, the Grand Constitutions of 1786 and the ritual of the eight added degrees, having been received in Charleston at that time. The bodies already established in Charleston, accepted the new regime and adopted the new degrees, and in 1801 a convention was held and preliminary steps inaugurated to form a Supreme Council of the

Thirty-third and Last Degree of the Ancient Accepted Scottish Rite of Freemasonry. The name of this new body was the Supreme Council of Sovereign Grand Inspectors General, of the Thirty-third and Last Degree for the United States of America. It was formed and organized by John Mitchel and Frederic Dalcho, and during the year the full number of members, nine, were admitted. Mitchel was Sovereign Grand Commander. The new body recognized the Constitutions of 1762, the Secret Constitutions and the much-discussed Constitutions of 1786.

The first Supreme Council at Charleston, S. C., began its labors on May 31, 1801, and its jurisdiction covered all the United States of America until August 5, 1813, at which date the "Supreme Council of the Ancient, Accepted Scottish Rite of Freemasonry, for the Northern Jurisdiction of the United States," was established by Special Deputy Emmanuel de la Motta at New York. At a later period the seat of the Supreme Council was changed to Boston.

Spread Of The Rite.

Today there are Scottish Rite organizations in practically every state, territory and dependency of the United States. New York State alone has eight Consistories; eleven Chapters of Rose Croix; thirteen Councils Princes of Jerusalem and eighteen Lodges of Perfection.

There are Supreme Councils of the Ancient Accepted Scottish Rite, legitimate and recognized by

ANCIENT ACCEPTED SCOTTISH RITE

each other, as follows: United States, 2; France, Belgium, Ireland, Brazil, Peru, New Granada, England and Wales, Scotland, Uruguay, Argentine Republic, Italy, 3; Colon, Venezuela, Cuba, Mexico, Portugal, Chili, Central America, Hungary, Greece, Switzerland, Canada, Rome, 1; Egypt, Spain, Tunis, Dominican Republic, Turkey, Luxemburg.

With the growth and development of the Rite in the United States, it was natural that Syracuse, which has long been an active Masonic center, should early have become interested in the Scottish Rite. Before the Civil War, a Lodge, Council, Chapter and Consistory were in operation, their jurisdiction taking in all of Western New York. It was there and in Rochester that the Buffalo Brethren received the Ineffable, Historical, Philosophical and Chivalric grades and it was there also that the inspiration, which resulted in Buffalo's present important Scottish Rite organization, was born. Following the organization of Buffalo Consistory, came that of Corning Consistory, and today the jurisdiction of the Buffalo higher body extends half way to Rochester on the North, and half way to Corning, in the Southern tier of counties of the State. Lodges of Perfection are in successful operation in Niagara Falls, Jamestown and Olean, their members obtaining the higher grades in Buffalo Consistory. The two latter have Councils of Princes of Jerusalem.

BUFFALO CONSISTORY, A. A. S. R.

Second Largest Body of the Rite in New York State, and a Social Center.

SCOTTISH Rite Masonry has reached in this city, a high degree of importance and influence. Occupying, in its own home in Delaware Avenue, over half a block along that beautiful thoroughfare, between West Huron and West Mohawk Streets, Buffalo Consistory is not only one of the largest bodies of 32d degree Masons in the country, but one of the most successful, as it is the most active, among the fraternal and social organizations of the State. Second only in point of membership to the great New York City Consistory, it comes even nearer to the front in the comprehensiveness of its work, in the completeness of its equipment and in the devotion of its members. It leads all in its social and educational activities.

It includes in its membership roll now, as it has during its entire life, a majority of the citizens of Buffalo of Masonic faith, who have risen to prominence in the social, business, political and official circles of Western New York. Its handsome property, conveniently situated on Buffalo's principal residential street, is the pride of its members and the envy of visiting patrons of the fraternity.

ANCIENT ACCEPTED SCOTTISH RITE

Not only is it the shrine where a constant procession of Brother Masons go to be enlightened in the higher principles of the great order; to study more thoroughly the precepts of fraternity and brotherly love entirely compatible with Divine teachings; but there, also, are provided the comforts, even luxuries of the typical fraternal "Home," where the tired pilgrim may find comfort, recreation and rest.

Initial Hardships.

To relate the history of Buffalo Consistory of the Ancient Accepted Scottish Rite, is to tell a story of initial hardships, disappointments and failures, lightened only by partial success, but coming finally, by thorough, earnest, well-applied effort and unselfish loyalty, to the highest plane of achievement. For this success, commendation must go, not alone to the first officers, who builded better than they knew; not fully to the men who have shaped the destiny of the organization in recent years, but in generous measure to the rank and file, who in their faithful devotion, have contributed of their best efforts to supplement the ambitious plans of their superior officers, by patient, conscientious and unselfish performance of the tasks assigned them, in the general distribution of the work.

When it is considered that all the degrees of Scottish Rite Masonry, from the 4th to the 32d inclusive, are conferred with full form and ceremony in the Consistory Cathedral in Delaware

Avenue, some idea of the number of people required for the work and the degree of loyalty demanded from the members, may be imagined. In some of the degrees as high as 117 individual characters are presented. To make the work fully effective, costumes and paraphernalia representing a value of over thirty thousand dollars are available, and the mechanical and electrical effects, are all that could be desired.

So, it will be seen, Fraternity has more than a superficial meaning in the case of Buffalo Consistory. Not only is it the Masonic shrine of an army of earnest, thoughtful, representative men, but as a tax-payer, it is turning into the city treasury a substantial sum every year.

At The Beginning.

In writing a history of Buffalo Consistory one must go back to the beginning, for it is upon this beginning, upon the foundation, strong and broad and deep, laid by the early craftsmen in the Valley of Buffalo, that the glory of the present Masonic edifice rests. Scottish Rite Masonry is composed of four distinct bodies, known as Lodge of Perfection, Council Princes of Jerusalem, Chapter of Rose Croix and Consistory.

After the Blue Lodge, the gateway of all Masonry, the Lodge of Perfection presents the first higher step in the attainment of the Ineffable Grades of the Scottish Rite. It includes the degrees from the 4th to the 14th inclusive, and may reasonably be credited with being a continuation,

ILL. WILLIAM HOMAN, 33°, ACTIVE
DEPUTY OF SUPREME COUNCIL FOR STATE OF NEW YORK AND
MOST ILLUSTRIOUS COMMANDER-IN-CHIEF OF THE
COUNCIL OF DELIBERATION

and completion, of the Blue Lodge work of Free and Accepted Masonry.

Up to 1867 there was no Scottish Rite organization in this State west of Rochester. Several Buffalo Masons, among whom were George C. Pennell, Robert T. Hayes, Christopher G. Fox and others, whose names will appear later, had taken the Lodge of Perfection degrees in either Syracuse or Rochester, and believed that there was a field for the Rite in this city. Early in 1867, application was made to the Supreme Council for a dispensation for the organization of Palmoni Lodge of Perfection and Palmoni Council, Princes of Jerusalem. This was granted and later in the same year, a charter was issued and the new Lodge and Council constituted, consecrated and dedicated, by officers of the Supreme Council and of Syracuse Consistory.

RECORD IS OBSCURE.

The history of Palmoni Lodge for the first sixteen years of its existence, or until 1883, is shrouded in the obscurity of nearly forgotten things. From the legends handed down by its founders, we know that its progress was slow, being hampered by opposition and obstructions of various character. The members of that little devoted band of ten, who sought to erect a permanent Scottish Rite shrine in the Valley of Buffalo, have, with one exception, answered the summons of the Grand Architect of the Universe, and can tell us nothing of those early struggles. A majority of the officers and members of the Lodge and Council, were engaged in occupations which prevented regular, or even frequent, attendance at the meetings. In reality, Palmoni Lodge was little more than a name, so far as active dissemination of Masonic light and knowledge are concerned, though maintaining its organization and adding an occasional name to its membership list, with limited form and ceremony, for there was no elaborate paraphernalia at hand, and few Brothers who were able to give to the work that attention, which its impressive presentation and exemplification demands.

All books and records which would be so valuable now, were destroyed in the fire of 1882, in the Miller and Greiner building, Washington and North Division Streets. The original charter, granted by the Supreme Council in 1867 was also lost at this time. For a long period the work of Lodge and Council was conducted under a special dispensation. In September, 1888, however, a duplicate Charter was issued by the Grand Body, which is still in possession of Palmoni Lodge. From this duplicate Charter we learn that the original charter members were the following:

First Charter List.

George C. Pennell, John W. Houghtailing, John H. Tryon, William S. Sizer, Christopher G. Fox, George H. Van Vleck, William Mullen, Robert P. Hayes, Henry Waters and F. H. Atkinson.

Of these ten original members, Christopher G. Fox was the last to lay down the working tools of life, his death occurring on September 12, 1912. Brother William Mullen, the only survivor of that little band of Scottish Rite pioneers in the Valley of Buffalo, is hale and hearty at the age of eighty-four. He regards as wonderful the remarkable success which has come to Palmoni Lodge and the higher bodies of the Rite, in these later years. Although no longer active in the Craft, his interest remains strong and his sympathies earnest.

From the records of the Supreme Council, we find that the first elected officers of Palmoni Lodge were:

George C. Pennell	*Thrice Potent Master*
Henry Waters	*Deputy Grand Master*
Robert P. Hayes	*Senior Grand Warden*
William Mullen	*Junior Grand Warden*
Charles E. Young	*Grand Orator*
George H. Van Vleck	*Grand Treasurer*
Origen S. Storrs	*Grand Secretary*
Christopher G. Fox	*Grand Master of Ceremonies*
John H. Tryon	*Grand Captain of the Guard*
John C. Graves	*Grand Hospitaler*
William S. Prior	*Grand Tiler*

There was a total membership of twenty-one.

Some Personal History.

Of that little band of ten, whose names were favorably considered by the Supreme Council, as worthy to be trusted with the charter of a new Lodge of the Rite, today, only one remains. The writer found this lone survivor remarkably well preserved in body and clear in mind, at his home

No. 65, the Circle, and for an hour enjoyed his reminiscences of the days when Scottish Rite Masonry was struggling, against strongly adverse circumstances, to gain a foothold in the Valley of Buffalo. Although not extremely active in Masonic work, at the time of Palmoni Lodge's organization, owing to the fact that his occupation, that of railroad conductor, prevented regular attendance at the communications of the Lodge, William Mullen remembers, with wonderful vividness, the associates who composed the original charter list of the proposed Lodge, and those who were chiefly responsible for the measure of success it attained.

Aside from the fact that he was a member of the original charter list of Palmoni Lodge, Brother Mullen's personal history is of value in this connection. Born in Ireland in 1832, William Mullen was brought to America by his parents, at the age of seven. He has been a resident of Buffalo for 63 years. On the 15th of June, 1852, he entered the service of the New York Central railroad as brakeman and was later promoted to the position of baggagemaster, and finally, conductor. He was in charge of the first stock-train run out of Buffalo, later becoming a passenger conductor, running between Buffalo and Syracuse up to the time of his retirement from the road. He is doubtless the oldest living railroad man in the Empire State.

Templars Alone Eligible.

Brother Mullen was raised to the sublime degree of Master Mason in Ancient Landmarks

ANCIENT ACCEPTED SCOTTISH RITE

Lodge, No. 441, F. & A. M., in 1865, in the administration of Worshipful John B. Sackett, as Master. He was exalted in Adytum Chapter, No. 235, Royal Arch Masons, in the following year and later received the Templar degrees in Hugh de Payens Commandery, No. 30. With the introduction of Scottish Rite Masonry into the Valley of Buffalo, it was made a condition of availability, that a candidate for admission to Palmoni Lodge of Perfection should be a Knight Templar. This provision of the by-laws continued until the reorganization after the disastrous fire, and was doubtless one of the causes, responsible for the slow growth of the new Body. In extending the privilege of membership to all worthy Master Masons, increased interest was stimulated, but the action also served to alienate the activities of certain of the earlier members, who had been earnest in their efforts to build up the Scottish Rite in Western New York, but who believed that the York and Scottish Rites should be in effect synonymous. That is the reason why certain names, prominently associated with the Lodge in its beginning, or in its earlier days, do not appear in the later chronicles.

Brother Mullen tells us that the Lodge of Perfection degrees of the Rite were received by the members of the original charter list, in Syracuse, and that he was in charge of the train which took them on that memorable pilgrimage. Later Rochester became the Mecca where the advanced mysteries were communicated to the Buffalo brethren. Brother Mullen holds life membership certificates from both the Lodge of the Ancient Landmarks and Adytum Chapter. He is a member of the United Presbyterian church and carries his eighty-four years with remarkable vigor.

Other Charter Members.

In this connection, it is interesting to note some of the characteristics of the nine men associated with Brother Mullen, in the organization of Palmoni Lodge. As has been said, all were members of the York Rite, and enrolled as Knights Templar, either in Hugh de Payens, or Lake Erie Commanderies. Most of them had also received the 32d Degree of the Scottish Rite.

George C. Pennell, the first Thrice Potent Master, was an Episcopal clergyman, being pastor of Grace Church in Niagara Street, and later of St. James. He was a member of the Scottish Rite before coming to Buffalo, but in what jurisdiction his membership was held, the writer has been unable to learn. He joined Hugh de Payens Commandery, and was Prior of that body for some time. Although active as a Mason, the Rite was considered by him, apparently, more a diversion than a serious proposition. Pennell was a man of prodigious strength. He weighed three hundred pounds and his capacity for social enjoyment was commensurate with his bulk. Many anecdotes of his physical power are related by those who knew him when he was at his best. It is said that he could take two of his men parishoners, one in either hand, and hold them out at arm's length with little apparent effort. His most important Masonic public work, as Master of Palmoni Lodge, was his assistance at the laying of the corner stone of the State Normal School at Fredonia.

John W. Houghtailing, like William Mullen, was a passenger conductor on the New York Central, or rather what is now a part of the New York Central system, the Lake Shore. His home was on North Division Street. He was not active in the work of the Craft, evidently owing to his occupation, which interferred with regular attendance.

John H. Tryon was a popular, well-liked citizen and brother. He was appointed first Captain of the Guard, in Palmoni Lodge, but there is nothing to indicate that he ever received advancement from that position.

A Landmark.

William S. Sizer, although an active member of the new Lodge, held no office in the organization. His time was fully occupied with his manufacturing business, in which he was very successful. He was the proprietor of the Sizer foundry. His home was on Niagara Square, in the building formerly occupied by Spencer Kellogg as an office. Mrs. Sizer is still living in Ferry Street.

George H. Van Vleck, first Grand Treasurer, was a successful oil operator in the Pennsylvania district. He was a man of remarkable business capacity, but was not particularly active in the Craft. He built a handsome home in Delaware

Avenue, on the site where now stands the Charles W. Goodyear residence.

Robert P. Hayes, who was the first Senior Grand Warden, was an enthusiastic Mason, an energetic and capable worker in the various bodies. He was the first High Priest of Adytum Chapter, serving in that capacity in 1869-70-71. He was connected with the United States Express Company and was later transferred to New York city, taking a more responsible place with the same company.

Henry Waters, first Deputy Master of Palmoni Lodge was active in the work of the Blue Lodge, being a member of Hiram Lodge, No. 105, F. & A. M., and its Master in 1866; High Priest of Buffalo Chapter, R. A. M. 1867-8, Master Buffalo Council 1877-8. He also was an employe of the New York Central railroad. He was killed in the fall of the roof of the old station. Brother Waters was a most proficient ritualist and was popular in Lodge, Chapter, Council and Commandery. He was a member of Lake Erie.

Charles E. Young was senior member of the firm of Young & Lockwood, stationers. He also was an active Mason and was made the first Grand Orator of Palmoni Lodge. He was for several years a most energetic and influential member of the Erie County Board of Supervisors. He was the fourth Master, of the Lodge of the Ancient Landmarks, serving in 1863-4. He was prominent in other Masonic circles. His home was on West Tupper Street. He held at one time the position of Grand Senior Deacon of the Grand Lodge.

WILLIAM MULLEN, 32°
ONLY SURVIVING MEMBER OF THE ORIGINAL CHARTER LIST OF PALMONI
LODGE OF PERFECTION. RESIDES AT No. 65, THE CIRCLE

Christopher G. Fox, is and was so closely associated in fact and in memory with Masonry in the State of New York, as to make extended notice of his activities superfluous in this connection. He was particularly energetic in the York Rite, and his name appears prominently in the records of all the various bodies of that Rite. There is nothing to indicate that he was equally active in the Scottish Rite, though he was appointed the first Master of Ceremonies of Palmoni Lodge. He was Master of Queen City Lodge, No. 358, from 1859 to 1862 inclusive and Commander of Hugh de Payens from 1864 to 1867 and from 1872 to 1878 inclusive. He served as High Priest of Keystone Chapter in 1858 and from 1867 to 1871 inclusive. He was for many years Grand Secretary of the Grand Chapter, Royal Arch Masons.

Palmoni's First Home.

The first meeting of Palmoni Lodge, under dispensation, was held in Washington Lodge rooms, at that time located in a building in Main Street, just South of Court Street. Shortly after that it moved to the Townsend Block, at Main and Swan Streets, where it remained until the Masonic Hall was removed to the Miller & Greiner Block, in Washington Street.

The first sixteen years of Lodge and Council, as observed above, were marked by stress and struggle, owing to various causes. Starting with ten members in 1867, it had increased only to 68 in 1882. The accessions to its roll, however, were of the progressive, broad-minded sort, and what was lacking in numbers and equipment, was to a degree offset, by earnest tenacity of purpose. Though the growth was small, it was of a lasting quality. To add to the trials with which the local founders of the Rite were forced to contend, the new organization was thrice scourged by fire, in which the records of the Lodge and Council were blotted out, the Charter and paraphernalia destroyed, leaving the Body practically destitute. In the last fire, which occurred on March 15, 1887, the organization was somewhat crippled, but the books and records accumulated after the previous disaster, were fortunately saved.

After The Fire.

Following the fire of 1882, there was a reorganization of the Lodge. At the meeting called for that purpose, only fourteen members responded. They were: A. Oppenheimer, Mark W. Cole, W. A. Woodson, Horace A. Noble, S. M. Every, James McCredie, Matthew Thielen, George H. Clarke, O. G. Nichols, Charles R. Dunning, Eugene S. Knapp, H. Klein, James A. Given and Henry Smith, 2d. From this time onward, the fortunes of Palmoni Lodge appear to have improved, though it was not until 1891, that evidences of real prosperity and promise of continued and satisfactory growth, were fully realized.

Much of this success must be credited to Abram Oppenheimer, whose earnest and persistent efforts to stimulate interest in the Scottish Rite, among local Masons, was productive of results. Brother Oppenheimer was Thrice Potent Master of the Lodge, from the reorganization in 1883, until 1886, and during that period, in which the degrees were exemplified in full form for the first time, forty-five candidates were initiated.

Mark W. Cole was Master during 1886 and there was no increase of membership. In 1887 and 1888, with George L. Kingston as Master, eleven candidates were instructed in the mysteries of the Rite, but without full ceremony, the degrees being communicated.

But sentiment created during the preceding years, began to take practical form, when Abram Oppenheimer was again called to preside during 1889 and 1890. During the two years seventy-six new names were added to the membership roll. Oppenheimer had realized that if interest was to be maintained, the degrees must be presented in full form and ceremony, and to this end, strenuous efforts were made to equip the Lodge with necessary paraphernalia and to drill the officers in their respective duties.

From that time, down to the present, the progress of Palmoni Lodge and Palmoni Council has been most flattering. A more detailed record of the work of each, through the succeeding years, will be found under appropriate heading. It is unfortunate that the list of those who served as officers during the time between 1867 and 1883, is unavailable. It is presumable, however, that those who assisted at the birth of the Scottish Rite infant in the Valley of Buffalo, were mainly responsible for the accomplishment of its early days; that their hands guided the rather puny child in its first somewhat uncertain steps.

CONSISTORY AND CHAPTER

Development of Palmoni Lodge. Results in Organization of Two Higher Bodies of the Rite in Buffalo.

ON January 28, 1892, Palmoni Lodge relinquished its quarters in the Austin Building and moved to the new Masonic Temple in Niagara street which had just been completed. Its membership had increased so substantially that the leading men of the lodge, who had taken the Consistory degrees in Rochester, felt justified in promoting a movement for the organization of the higher body in the Valley of Buffalo. Accordingly, in September of that year, Ill. Charles W. Cushman, 33°, Thrice Potent Master, accompanied by Ill. David L. Day, 33°, attended the session of the Supreme Council held in Providence, R. I., to urge the granting of a dispensation for a Buffalo Chapter of Rose Croix and Consistory. Some slight objection was interposed by the brethren of the Rochester Consistory, who realized the loss in membership they were likely to sustain if a higher body of the Rite should be established in this end of the state, but this objection was readily overcome, and on December 8, 1892, letters of dispensation were granted, for the establishment of Buffalo Consistory, S. P. R. S., and Buffalo Chapter of Rose Croix, H. R. D. M.

HISTORY OF BUFFALO CONSISTORY

On January 1, 1893, Illustrious Brother Cushman, who had been honored with the distinction of being the first member of the Supreme Council of the 33° Active, from the Valley of Buffalo, retired as Master of Palmoni Lodge of Perfection, for the purpose of devoting his efforts more completely to the interests of the new body. He was succeeded by Brother George L. Brown. On January 6th, was held the first rendezvous of Buffalo Consistory, in Masonic Hall. The officers under dispensation were Charles W. Cushman, 33°, Illustrious Commander-in-Chief; Charles A. DeLaney, 1st Lieutenant-Commander and Francis G. Ward, 2d Lieutenant-Commander. The other sublime princes whose names appeared on the dispensation, were:

Under Dispensation.

Jacob Stern, Frank S. Coit, John L. Brothers, Matthew Theilen, Henry Smith, 2d, George L. Brown, Tellico Johnson, M. G. Weber, Frank Hammond, Charles DeLaney, William M. Bloomer, Samuel Root, Charles R. Fitzgerald, Clark W. Rice, George J. H. Goehler, Frank T. Haggerty, Robert T. Walker, Fred William Fisher, Wilber N. Hoag, James L. Walker, George H. Young, Robert C. Titus, Andrew Shiels, Eugene S. Knapp, George L. Kingston, Abram Oppenheimer, Louis P. Adolff, Jr., Charles J. Close, A. F. Miller, Joseph H. Horton, George H. Clarke, Charles E. Markham, Will H. Dick, W. J. Cronyn, H. G. Falke, Henry Schaefer, James C. Holliday, Joel

H. Prescott, George R. Wolfe, Arthur L. Knight, George Reiman, J. L. Whittet, E. E. Coatsworth, John Malcolm, William J. Runcie, W. H. Rice, Ole E. Goldhagen, Orin G. Nichols, Henry G. Knapp, W. L. Alexander, James Chalmers, Theodore L. Wadsworth.

At this meeting the first three officers named in the dispensation were endorsed and the following subordinate officers elected: W. L. Alexander, Minister of State; W. J. Cronyn, Grand Chancellor; Samuel Root, Treasurer, Theodore L. Wadsworth, Secretary; Tellico Johnson, Engineer and Architect; Andrew Shiels, Hospitaler; Clark W. Rice, Master of Ceremonies; Will H. Dick, Grand Standard Bearer; Charles J. Close, Captain of the Guard; John Malcolm, Sentinel.

At the third meeting of the new Consistory, the first petitions for membership were received and approved. The candidates whose names were thus first to be added to the roll of fifty-five, a roll which was destined to reach unprecedented proportions among the Scottish Rite bodies of the State, were Fred Erfling, J. W. Chatman, William Page and Albert T. Brown. All the degrees from the 4th to the 32d inclusive, were communicated. At the following meeting held on May 26, 1893, the four new members were appointed choristers, with Robert Denton, organist. At this meeting petitions were received from thirty-four candidates who had already received the degrees of the three lower bodies.

HISTORY OF BUFFALO CONSISTORY

On May 31st, the fifth meeting of the energetic members of Buffalo Consistory was held, and the petitions of forty-eight prospective candidates received. This meeting had special significance and interest to the members, for it was the first at which any of the beautiful degrees was conferred in full form and ceremony, it being that of Patriarch Noachite, or Prussian Knight. From this time forward, however, the unflagging zeal of the officers, especially the Commander-in-Chief, was successful in equipping the young Consistory with the necessary paraphernalia and increasing facilities for the work. This, combined with the great interest manifested by the capable and ambitious members, enabled Illustrious Commander Cushman, from that time forward, to increase with pleasing rapidity, the number of degrees to be exemplified in full form, and thus assure rapid and substantial growth. Under dispensation two degrees only were thus worked—the 21st and 30th.

COLONEL WARD PRESIDED.

At the meeting held on September 22, 1893, at which Second Lieutenant-Commander, Francis G. Ward, presided for the first time, a letter was received from Commander-in-Chief Cushman, then in attendance at the annual meeting of the Supreme Council in Chicago, containing the pleasing news, that charters had been granted, creating Buffalo Chapter of Rose Croix, and Buffalo Consistory. Arrangements were at once begun for the proper reception of the Supreme Council offi-

ABRAM OPPENHEIMER, 32°
FIRST THRICE POTENT MASTER OF PALMONI LODGE OF PERFECTION,
FOLLOWING THE REORGANIZATION IN 1883, AFTER THE BIG FIRE

cers, who would come to Buffalo to present the charter and institute the new organization. This important duty devolved upon Ill. John Hodge, 33° Active, Deputy for the State of New York, his chief assistant being Ill. David F. Day. The ceremonies of institution were conducted in the Scarlet Room of the Masonic Temple, on Friday evening, November 24, 1893, in the presence of 118 officers and members. A single substitution had been made in the charter, as compared with the original list of officers named in the dispensation, Robert C. Titus taking the place of W. J. Cronyn, as Grand Chancellor.

First Triennial Election.

The first triennial election of Buffalo Consistory was held on December 18, 1896. At this meeting Charles E. Markham was elected secretary, although he had been acting in that capacity, following the annual reunion on March 25th of that year. From an address delivered by the Commander-in-Chief at the December meeting, we learn something of the satisfactory growth of the baby organization during the first three years of its existence. It shows that the classes elevated to the degree of Prince of the Royal Secret, at each of the intervening annual reunions, at which alone the 32d degree was conferred, were as follows: First reunion, in May, 1893, while under dispensation, 82; second reunion 1894, 56; third, 1895, 72; fourth, 1896, 43, a total of 253. The total membership at the time of the first triennial election was 390. During the three years, death had chosen for its victims ten of the members of Buffalo Consistory.

The Character Of Mason.

In presenting this brief history of Buffalo Consistory and the progress of Scottish Rite Masonry in the Valley of Buffalo, we feel that the general public should be enlightened to a degree regarding the aims, principles and teachings of this great fraternal organization. This can be done no more clearly, or impressively, than by quoting from the address of the late lamented Commander-in-Chief, the Illustrious Brother Charles W. Cushman, on the occasion referred to above. Appealing to the members, he said:

"Let me impress upon your minds, Princes, that the uppermost grade among true Masons, is that of gentleman. It does not matter how many degrees a brother has taken, or how many orders have been conferred upon him, he still lacks the highest, unless he can prove himself to be the true gentleman. There are certain unerring tests by which to decide. It is to be forbearing and gentle, careful of the feelings of others; to be above personal spite, malice and vindictiveness; to be courteous, magnanimous and considerate. If we show these and other like qualities; believe me, we may be regarded as true men. Every faithful citizen is, I am sure, desirous of attaining this highest grade and give tangible expression of the graces and virtues that ennoble manhood."

Coming from a man, who in his daily walk truly exemplified the principles he so earnestly and faithfully taught in his Consistory work, such words could not fail to make a deep and lasting impression. Buffalo Consistory today, blesses the fate which brought to control of its early destinies, a man of the type of Charles W. Cushman.

Patriotic Impulses.

A further digression may be permissible to speak of the patriotic impulses with which Scottish Rite Masonry is inspired; the loyalty to country which finds expression each year on the occasion of Flag Day, when Consistory members congregate in the early morning hours to pay their respects to the National ensign. Buffalo Consistory raised the Stars and Stripes at its third annual reunion, placing it beside its own banner. In referring to the incident, Ill. Brother Cushman said:

"It cannot be possible that this Consistory will step backward, while that flag floats over us, its stars representing the starry pavilion over the world; its blue the broad canopy of Heaven; its red the bright sunshine of the morning and its white the purity of God's innocence. We will march on united under one flag and one God; under one standard of right and honesty, to renewed prosperity and happiness."

Such were the predominant impulses of the Father of Scottish Rite Masonry in its highest degrees, in Buffalo; impulses which have been equally characterized by his successors in the high office of Commander-in-Chief, Ill. Brother Francis G. Ward, 33°, and Ill. Brother George K. Staples,

33°, the present efficient head of the organization. These principles, injected into the blood of the baby Consistory, have gone far to induce the healthy growth and to develop the great but symetrical fraternal giant, whose home in Delaware Avenue is the surprise and admiration of all visiting brothers.

An Early Recruit.

An important meeting, as regards its influence upon the future of Buffalo Consistory, was that of March 30, 1898. On that date, along with twenty-nine other Knights of the Rose Croix, appeared George Kelley Staples for his first introduction to the Consistory grades. Needless to observe, perhaps, that his personality was not so pronounced then, as now. Best evidence of the discretion of the investigating committee is found in the rapid advancement which came to the neophite, who, in 1910, was unanimously elected Master of Palmoni Lodge of Perfection. His record for the two years he held the key to the gateway of the Consistory, speaks for itself.

These digressions may seem like discordant notes, yet they are forced upon us by the incidents which they emphasize. They all have their direct bearing on the present importance of the subject under consideration.

Reunion Of 1899.

Buffalo Consistory has enjoyed many pleasant reunions, but probably none more expressive of the pleasure and appreciation of those inducted into its mysteries, than that of 1899. On this date, Ill. Brother Charles W. Cushman received first material testimonial, of the affection and esteem in which he was held by the members of the Scottish Rite in the Valley of Buffalo. At that time, in the closing hours of the reunion, all the workers in the various grades, as they had appeared in their parts, were grouped in the East, while Ill. Edward W. Hatch, 33°, in impressive language, presented to the loved Commander-in-Chief an elegant Commander's jewel. At the same time, Truman C. White, president of the class of 1899, presented, on behalf of the class, to the Ill. Commander-in-Chief of Buffalo Consistory; to Ill. John L. Brothers, 33°, Most Wise Master of Buffalo Chapter of Rose Croix; to Ill. Charles E. Hayes, 33°, Sovereign Prince of Palmoni Council Princes of Jerusalem and to Ill. Louis P. Adolf, 33°, Thrice Potent Master of Palmoni Lodge of Perfection, each a basket of flowers. The reunion closed with a banquet at the Hotel Iroquois, attended by 244 members.

The eleventh reunion, which opened on March 25, 1903, was memorable, as being the last meeting of Buffalo Consistory at which Ill. Charles W. Cushman presided. Failing health, continuing over a period of five years, had necessitated relinquishment by the Illustrious Brother of many of his Masonic duties, but he continued faithful and loyal to his lusty fraternal child, until the last. As the time for the regular fall resumption of the

Consistory work, approached, death came to the beloved Commander-in-Chief. He was called to cross the dark river on August 19, 1903, dying as he had lived, with strong confidence of the future and an unshaken faith in the bounteousness of God's mercy. To the younger members of Buffalo Consistory, and to those who are to come within its warming influence hereafter, a brief biography of the founder of the great organization in Buffalo, will prove of interest and value.

ILL. CHARLES W. CUSHMAN, 33°

Organizer and First Commander-in-Chief of Buffalo Consistory, Retaining the Office Ten Years.

BROTHER Cushman was born August 31, 1848, in Cleveland, O. He was educated in the public schools of that city and in the High School of Rockford, Ill. As a good Mason, Brother Cushman was patriotic, and at the age of 16, enlisted in an Illinois regiment, serving as a drummer during 1864 and 1865, a soldier in the Civil War. He was married on the 18th of March, 1873, to Georgia L. Doran, of Chicago. His widow and one son, William D. Cushman, for several years active in the Consistory work and a Past Most Wise Master of Buffalo Chapter of Rose Croix, at present a prosperous New York City attorney, survive him.

As a business man, Charles W. Cushman ranked high. He entered the service of the Lake Shore & Michigan Central Railway Company in 1869, the year of his majority, and three years later was made general agent of the company, a position he held until 1880. In the latter year he organized the Railway Car Association, of which he was president until the time of his death. He was also president of the Columbia Equipment Company, and of the Standard Iron Works, besides being a stockholder and director in various other business enterprises.

Ill. Brother Cushman's Masonic history was particularly brilliant; his work for the craft inspiring to others and of great benefit to the fraternity. He was made a Master Mason May 11, 1872, in Washington Lodge, No. 240, of Buffalo; a Royal Arch Mason on February 7, 1883, in Keystone Chapter, No. 163, Buffalo; a Royal and Select Master, in Keystone Council, No. 20, Buffalo, and a Knight Templar, December 10, 1883, in Hugh de Payens Commandery, No. 30, Buffalo.

In the Scottish Rite, he received the degrees from the 4th to the 14th inclusive, in Palmoni Lodge of Perfection, April 27, 1883; the 15th and 16th degrees, in Palmoni Council Princes of Jerusalem, on the same date in Buffalo; the 17th and 18th degrees, in Rochester Chapter of Rose Croix, March 19, 1884, and the 19th to the 32d degrees inclusive, in Rochester Consistory, March 20, 1884. Ten years later, September 18, 1894, he received the thirty-third degree in the Supreme Council in Boston, Mass., and was constituted an active member of the Supreme Council at Providence, R. I., on September 19, 1895.

His Guiding Hand.

From the time of the Consistory organization until the date of his death, eleven years, Brother Cushman's was the guiding hand which directed the bark of Scottish Rite Masonry, in safe and prosperous waters, in the Valley of Buffalo. But

ILL. CHARLES W. CUSHMAN, 33°
PRIME MOVER IN ITS ORGANIZATION AND COMMANDER-IN-CHIEF
OF BUFFALO CONSISTORY FOR THE FIRST TEN
YEARS OF ITS EXISTENCE

earnest as was his effort for the new organization, he continued his allegiance to his earlier Masonic attachment, the York Rite, and performed valuable work in Lodge, Chapter, Grand Chapter, Commandery and Grand Commandery. Nor was he a stranger in the Grand Lodge of the State. He was Junior Grand Warden in 1895, 1896, 1897 and 1898, and Senior Grand Warden from 1899 to 1901. At the session of the Grand Lodge, in the latter year, Brother Cushman was again elected Senior Grand Warden, by acclamation, but owing to failing health was obliged to decline the high honor.

Then the Grand Lodge took action which had not been paralleled in its history. Most Worshipful James Ten Eyck, Past Grand Master, presented the following, which was unanimously adopted:

"Appreciating the great service rendered the craft by R. W. Brother Cushman and deeply regretting that his physical condition compels him to decline the office of Senior Grand Warden;

"Resolved, That, as an expression of our esteem, Brother Charles W. Cushman be, and he is hereby, made Honorable Past Grand Master, with the title of 'Most Worshipful.'"

As a degree worker, Ill. Brother Cushman had few equals and no superiors. He created the character of Walraven in the 20th degree, giving to it remarkable effectiveness.

ANNUAL REUNIONS
Most Important Events in the History of Buffalo's Highest Scottish Rite Body.

RECORDING the annual reunions, regularly held by Buffalo Consistory, one secures a comprehensive idea of the vast amount of work which the officers and members have been called upon to perform, and the record clearly demonstrates the loyalty, unselfishness and zeal which have characterized the brethren, in their promulgation of the principles of the order, and the character of the Masonic ideals which they have set up.

To go back once more to the beginning, then, to the second annual reunion held, the date of institution counting as the first, we find that the meeting extended over two days, Friday and Saturday, March 30th and 31st, 1894. Fifty-three petitions for degrees and membership were received, and the applicants were inducted into the mysteries of the 19th, 20th, 21st, 22d, 23d, 24th, 25th, 26th, 27th, 28th and 29th degrees, the first three being exemplified in full form, the others communicated.

THIRD REUNION.

At the third reunion, which opened on Thursday evening, March 28, 1895, and continued until

Saturday evening, March 30th, the 32d degree, Prince of the Royal Secret, was conferred for the first time in Buffalo Consistory in full and ample form. Seventy-two candidates were members of the class. The 30th degree, Knight of the White and Black Eagle, was also exemplified in full form for the first time by the Buffalo brethren. Other degrees put on in full form at this reunion were the 20th and 21st.

In September, 1894, the first session in Buffalo, of the Supreme Council, was held, and Brothers Horace A. Noble, John L. Brothers, George L. Brown and Robert C. Titus were the recipients of the 33d and last degree. At a special meeting of the Consistory, held on Monday evening, November 18, 1895, for that purpose, Prince Edward W. Hatch, on behalf of the members, presented to the four brothers, the rings and jewels of their high station.

Fourth Reunion.

The fourth annual reunion opened on Wednesday afternoon, March 25, 1896, and continued with morning, afternoon and evening sessions until Friday. A class of 43 were received into the 19th, 20th, 21st, 29th and 32d degrees with full form and ceremony, the other degrees being communicated. A handsome floral piece was presented to the presiding officer by Prince Louis Rapin. A vote of thanks was tendered by the Consistory.

For some unexplained reason, the first triennial election of Buffalo Consistory was not held at the constitutional time, and it became necessary to secure from the Deputy for New York, Ill. Charles E. Ide, 33° Active, of Syracuse, a dispensation, permitting the body to hold its election in December. The dispensation was secured and forwarded by the Grand Secretary, Ill. Joseph P. Abel, 33° Active, of New York. Reference has already been made to this first triennial election, and quotation made from an address, presented at the time, by Commander-in-Chief Cushman. It is so good that we feel fully justified in borrowing from that address still further. Ill. Brother Cushman said:

"Masonry, which has withstood earth's changes; the shock of nations and revolutions of the ages; the hatred of misguided and misinformed men, will still live if we are true. Scepters pass away, thrones crumble, kingdoms fall, but the Masonic fabric will stand, if we are true, unchanged and unchanging. Masonry will exist unto the end of the ages, if we live up to our high privileges and exemplify without, what we are taught within; the beacon light that guides us by day and by night and illuminates our lives with its grandeur."

FIFTH REUNION.

On the fifth annual reunion, the work was for the first time extended over four days, commencing on Wednesday, March 30th, and closing on Friday evening, April 2d, 1897. Thirty-four candidates were received. At this reunion the number of degrees to be conferred in full form was reduced, owing to indisposition on the part of the Commander-in-Chief. He was however able to communicate the 32d degree to the class. It is of interest that the well-known newspaper correspondent, a former Buffalo editor, Samuel G. Blythe, was a member of this class. There were present as visitors the following members of the Supreme Council: Illustrious Brothers, Clinton F. Page, 33°, Brenton D. Babcock, 33°, E. J. Cutler, 33°, Commander-in-Chief of Cleveland Consistory and Charles R. Butler, 33°, also of Cleveland.

On May 14, 1897, a special meeting of Buffalo Consistory was held for the purpose of receiving the officers of the Council of Deliberation, the Supreme State body of the Scottish Rite. The Council of Deliberation is composed of the first three officers of each Consistory, the first three officers of each Chapter of Rose Croix, the first four officers of each Council Princes of Jerusalem and the first four officers of each Lodge of Perfection. It is presided over by the Deputy for the State, who holds the title of Most Illustrious Commander-in-Chief. At this time the 20th degree was exemplified in full form and ceremony, Prince Frank B. Hower presiding in the first section and Prince Francis G. Ward in the second section. Samuel G. Blythe was selected to impersonate the candidate. Illustrious Henry L. Palmer, Sovereign Grand Commander of the Northern Jurisdiction, was received on the grand honors and gave an eloquent address.

Sixth Annual Reunion.

At the Sixth Annual Reunion, held on March 29th, 30th, 31st, and April 1st, 1898, a class of thirty were enlightened respecting the mysteries of the order, including the 32d degree, which was conferred by Illustrious Commander Cushman, assisted by Lieutenant-Commander Charles A. DeLaney. Brother William Palmer, president of the class, presented to the Consistory and its Commander, a beautiful floral double eagle and a basket of roses.

Seventh Annual Reunion.

At the Seventh Annual Reunion, held on Wednesday, Thursday and Friday, March 29th, 30th and 31st, 1899, forty-eight candidates were received as Sublime Princes. This reunion was marked by the presence of a number of members of the Supreme Council, the following being in attendance.

Ill. Clinton F. Paige, 33°, Grand Secretary General; Ill. Brenton F. Babcock, 33°, Deputy for Ohio; Ill. William Gibson, 33°, of the Dominion of Canada; Ill. Erastus C. Delevan, 33°, Binghamton, N. Y.; Ill. George E. Newell, 33°, Medina; Ill. Edward R. Washburn, 33°, Brooklyn; Ill. Edward Paige, 33°, Cleveland, Ohio.

The second triennial election of Buffalo Consistory was held on Friday evening, December 22, 1898. The Ill. John L. Brothers was called by the Commander-in-Chief to preside and Ill. George L. Brown, and Prince E. K. Emery were appointed tellers. The following officers were chosen:

ANCIENT ACCEPTED SCOTTISH RITE

Ill. Charles W. Cushman	*Commander-in-Chief*
Francis G. Ward	*First Lieut.-Commander*
Charles E. Hayes	*Second Lieut.-Commander*
Joel H. Prescott, Jr.	*Minister of State*
Robert C. Titus	*Grand Chancellor*
Samuel Root	*Grand Treasurer*
Charles E. Markham	*Grand Secretary*
John Malcolm	*Grand Engineer and Architect*
Andrew Shiels	*Grand Hospitaler*
William H. Lyons	*Grand Master of Ceremonies*
Will H. Dick	*Grand Standard Bearer*
John T. Gard	*Grand Captain of the Guard*
George H. Young	*Grand Sentinel*

These officers were installed by Ill. John L. Brothers and associate officers.

Eighth Annual Reunion.

The Eighth Annual Reunion extended over three days, commencing at 4 o'clock, p. m., Wednesday, March 28, 1900. Forty petitioners were accepted and instructed in the various degrees. In this class were two men who have since held important offices in the lower bodies, and have contributed, generously and unselfishly of their time and talents, to assist in bringing Buffalo Consistory up to the high position it occupies among the bodies of the Scottish Rite. They were John Sutherland Embleton and Hugh Alexander Sloan. Among the distingushed guests present at this reunion, was Ill. John V. Ellis, 33°, Past Sovereign Commander of the Rite in the Dominion of Canada. Ill. Clinton F. Paige, 33°, Grand Secretary General, was elected by acclamation an honorary member of Buffalo Consistory.

At the regular meeting held on Friday evening, March 22, 1901, the Commander-in-Chief announced the death of Prince Theodore L. Wadsworth, the first secretary of the Consistory, he having been named in the charter and had served continuously, in both that and the co-ordinate bodies, up to January 26, 1896, when failing health had demanded his retirement. Brother Wadsworth had been of great assistance to his Commander-in-Chief during the early struggles of the new organization and was highly esteemed by the members. News of his death was received with deep regret, which found expression in a vote of sympathy and commiseration sent to the surviving relatives.

NINTH ANNUAL REUNION.

On March 27th, 28th and 29th, 1901, occurred the Ninth Annual Reunion, at which fifty candidates were instructed in the degrees. At this reunion, Walter Martin Zink, who has since proven himself one of the most efficient and untiring workers in the various degrees, and has served as Sovereign Prince in Palmoni Council, was made a Prince of the Royal Secret. Addresses were made by the Ill. Brothers, Clinton F. Paige, William A. Gibson and Edwin A. Washburn.

At a regular meeting of Buffalo Consistory held on Friday evening, November 22, 1901, Ill. Francis G. Ward, Lieutenant-Commander, presided, and at this meeting was received the first official order from Ill. William Homan, who had succeeded Ill.

ILL. ROBERT C. TITUS, 33°
ACTIVE MEMBER OF THE SUPREME COUNCIL; A CHARTER MEMBER OF
BUFFALO CONSISTORY AND ONE OF ITS FIRST TRUSTEES

ANCIENT ACCEPTED SCOTTISH RITE

Brother Ide to the New York state deputyship, and who was destined to become one of the most loyal admirers and helpful friends that the Buffalo Consistory has gained among the officers of the Supreme Council.

TENTH ANNUAL REUNION.

At the Tenth Annual Reunion which opened on Wednesday, March 26, 1902, sixty-nine petitions were received, among the candidates being two clergymen, the first members of the cloth to apply for admission. They were the Rev. Charles Edward Locke and the Rev. Vernum Pery Mather. There were present at this reunion a large number of visitors including eighteen members of the Grand Council, as follows:

Ill. Clinton F. Paige, 33°, Grand Secretary General for the Supreme Council; Ill. Hugh Murray, 33°, Grand Secretary General for the Northern jurisdiction of the United States; Ill. Henry M. Fisher, 33°, Grand Secretary General for the Dominion of Canada; Ill. John L. Lakin, 33°, Past Commander-in-Chief of Massachusetts Consistory; Ill. James A. Davis, 33°, also a Past Commander of the Massachusetts Consistory; Ill. Charles C. Hutchinson, 33°, Deputy for Massachusetts; Ill. Edwin C. Hall, 33°, Commander-in-Chief Central City Consistory; Ill. Thomas Brooks, 33°, Commander-in-Chief Rochester Consistory; and the Illustrious Brothers, George A. Newill, 33°, Medina; Americus V. Holmes, 33°, Arthur B. Wrigley, 33° and George B. Johnson, 33°, of Pittsburg; Jay B. Kline, 33°, Syracuse; William Gibson, 33°, Beamsville, Ont.; Charles R. Butler, 33°, Cleveland; N. K. Elliott, 33°, Indianapolis; John B. Coleman, 33°, Rochester. Ill. Charles W. Cushman presented to Ill. Freeman Clinton Paige, Grand Secretary General of the Supreme Council, an engrossed certificate of honorary membership in Buffalo Consistory. Brother Paige was Commander-in-Chief of Ossening Consistory of Binghamton. At the banquet which followed the reunion, at the Hotel Iroquois, 325 members and guests were present. At the first meeting following the summer vacation, the Ill. Commander-in-Chief was called to perform the unpleasant duty of announcing the death of Brother Paige, which occurred at his home in Binghamton, on November 13, 1902.

Third Triennial Election.

At the third triennial election held on December 26, 1902, all of the elective officers were returned to their previous stations. Among the appointive officers, all were retained, with the exception of John T. Gard, Grand Captain of the Guard, Charles N. Riggs being appointed in his stead. John W. Walker was appointed Organist and the office of Grand Prior established, Rt. Rev. Charles H. Fowler being appointed.

Eleventh Annual Reunion.

The Eleventh Annual Reunion, which opened on Wednesday, March 25, 1903, reflected the increasing interest which was obtaining among the brethren of the craft, in the Valley of Buffalo, concerning Scottish Rite Masonry. The class, which was to receive the 32d degree, consisted of eighty earnest citizens and Masons, whose love for the order inspired a desire for enlightenment in its higher mysteries. At this reunion the Ill. Commander-in-Chief enjoyed the great privilege of conferring the highest Consistory degree upon his only son, William D. Cushman, who was later to give to the body some of the energy which had marked his Illustrious father's Masonic career. This was Ill. Brother Cushman's last official service, his death occurring three months later, during the Summer vacation. Illustrious brothers were present from Albany, Cleveland, Rochester, Beamsville, Ont., Syracuse, Troy, Detroit, Palmyra, Medina, and Elizabeth, N. J. Three hundred and sixty-nine members and guests banqueted together, following the reunion's closing session.

A Great Loss.

At the regular meeting held on Friday evening, November 27, 1903, the dark shadow of an inexpressible sorrow rested upon the members. On the 19th of August of that year, their beloved Commander-in-Chief had been numbered with the mighty host gone to explore that unknown country, thus for the first time breaking the continuous official record of the Consistory which had continued over a period of twelve years, with uninterrupted and ever increasing success. By authority of a special order issued by Ill. William Homan, 33° Active, Deputy of the Supreme Council for the State of New York, Ill. Brother John L. Brothers, 33°, presided.

Following the regular business meeting, there was held on the same evening, under special dispensation issued by Ill. Deputy Homan, on request of Ill. Francis G. Ward, 33°, acting Commander-in-Chief, an election to fill vacancies. Ill. Francis G. Ward was chosen Commander-in-Chief, Ill. Joel H. Prescott, 33°, First Lieutenant-Commander and Ill. George L. Brown, 33°, Minister of State, to fill vacancy caused by the advancement of Ill. Brother Prescott. These officers were installed by Ill. John L. Brothers, acting Commander-in-Chief. At the earlier meeting of the evening, there was received a petition for affiliation from a brother who was later to become the head of one of the co-ordinate bodies, Charles Henry Andrews. Brother Andrews had been a member of Oakland Consistory, No. 2, of California.

Twelfth Annual Reunion.

On April 6, 1904, was opened the Twelfth Annual Reunion, the first at which Ill. Francis G. Ward presided as Commander-in-Chief. At this reunion there was received the largest class in the history of the Consistory up to that time, though it was only an earnest of the gigantic strides the organization was destined to make, later on. In fact, the class of 1904 was just double, in its membership, any that had preceded it, numbering 116.

ANCIENT ACCEPTED SCOTTISH RITE

Included in the list were three more brothers who were immediately to identify themselves with the active working forces of the Consistory—one to become the chief support and dependence of the Commander-in-Chief, in the most trying parts. They were George A. Halbin, Peter F. Piper and Albert Hatch Zink. Of Brother Zink's remarkable and versatile talents we shall have more to say later on. The following degrees were conferred in full form and ceremony: 19th, Grand Pontiff, Ill. Edward W. Hatch, 33°, presiding. 20th, Master AdVitum, Prince George Clinton, 32° presiding in first section; Ill. Francis G. Ward, 33°, second section. Twenty-first, Prussian Knight, Ill. John L. Brothers, 33°, presiding. Twenty-fifth, Knight of the Brazen Serpent, Prince Howard D. Herr, 32°, presiding. Twenty-seventh, Commander of the Temple, Prince Otto Volger, 32°, presiding first section, Prince Louis W. Marcus, 32°, second section. Twenty-ninth, Knight of St. Andrew, Prince Frank T. Gilbert, 32°, presiding; Thirty-second, Prince of the Royal Secret, Ill. Francis G. Ward presiding.

Commander-in-Chief Francis G. Ward presented to the Consistory a handsome oil painting of the late Ill. Charles W. Cushman, procured by the committee appointed for that purpose. Sixteen Illustrious Brothers were in attendance at the reunion from Troy, Brooklyn, Albany, Corning, Binghamton, Rochester, and Beamsville, Toronto and Hamilton, in Ontario. Ill. Charles M. Heald, late of Michigan, who had just taken up his residence in Buffalo and who was to become one of the first councilmen of this city under the commission form of government, made his first visit to Buffalo Consistory on this occasion.

Seeking New Home.

Another meeting which had a strong bearing upon the fortunes of Buffalo Consistory, was that of October 28, 1904. Ill. Joel H. Prescott, First Lieutenant-Commander, presided in the absence of the Commander-in-Chief. Ill. Francis G. Ward was elected to the board of directors to fill vacancy caused by the death of Ill. Charles W. Cushman. A resolution was adopted appointing a committee, consisting of Ill. Francis G. Ward, Ill. Robert C. Titus and Ill. Joel H. Prescott, with power "to negotiate and contract for the purchase of the Unitarian Church property in Delaware Avenue, at a price not to exceed $35,000." Another resolution was adopted authorizing the trustees to "take title to the property known as the 'Unitarian Church of Our Father,' situated on Delaware Avenue, and to give a bond and mortgage for twenty thousand dollars, a portion of the purchase price of said property, and to do all such other things, and incur such expenses as may be necessary, to perfect the title in the Consistory."

At the succeeding meeting, held on November 25, of the same year, the Commander-in-Chief announced the purchase of the property and explained that the necessary fund for making re-

ANCIENT ACCEPTED SCOTTISH RITE

quired alterations would be raised by subscription. He also reported that possession of the auditorium would be given on December 26th and of the entire church property on or before January 1, 1905. A committee composed of Ill. Robert C. Titus, Ill. Joseph Fowler and Ill. John L. Brothers was appointed to draw papers and incorporate Buffalo Consistory in accordance with the act governing fraternal bodies. At the last meeting of the year, and the last in the Masonic Temple in Niagara Street, held on December 23d, among the petitions presented was that of Charles Elbert Rhodes, present Most Wise Master of Palmoni Chapter of Rose Croix.

THIRTEENTH ANNUAL REUNION.

The Thirteenth Annual Reunion, the last to be held in the Masonic Temple, opened on Wednesday, April 26, 1905. Owing to the great amount of work incident to a remodeling of the acquired property in Delaware Avenue, to make the somewhat ancient building suitable for the proper exemplification of the Consistory degrees, an extension of the lease of the rooms which had been headquarters for the Scottish Rite Masons so long, had been obtained. On the last day of the reunion, one hundred and seven candidates were members of the class to receive the 32d degree, Prince of the Royal Secret, it being conferred in full form. Distingushed guests were present from Beamsville, Sarnia, and Hamilton, Ont., Jersey City, N. J. and Medina, N. Y.

HISTORY OF BUFFALO CONSISTORY

At a regular meeting of the Consistory, held on Friday evening, October 27, 1905, steps were taken for a proper incorporation of Buffalo Consistory, to enable it to "legally take and convey such real and personal property as may be necessary for the transaction of its business and the promotion of the interests of the order." Three years previously articles of incorporation had been adopted, but it was found that an error had been made, the instrument having been drawn under the wrong statute, not under the one providing for the incorporation of benevolent orders. On motion of Ill. Brother George L. Brown, a resolution was adopted providing:

"That the proper officers of this Consistory, proceed to take the necessary steps to procure a proper incorporation of this body.

"Resolved: That three trustees be elected by ballot, as provided by law to be named in said certificate as the Trustees thereof, and that said officers be and they are hereby authorized and directed to execute and file a further amended or supplemental certificate of incorporation, and that said certificate, heretofore filed, be abandoned and surrendered as the Charter of this order and that all corporate rights and privileges acquired thereunder, so as to completely and perfectly obtain all the rights and privileges granted and provided by Chapter 377, of the laws of 1896, as fully and completely as though said original certificate had not been made and filed."

ELECTION OF TRUSTEES.

An election was then held for the selection of the three Trustees provided by the law, to serve

ILL. CHARLES E. MARKHAM, 33°
SECRETARY OF BUFFALO CONSISTORY AND CO-ORDINATE BODIES
FROM 1896 UNTIL HIS DEATH IN 1910

under the Act of Incorporation. Ill. Francis G. Ward, Ill. Joel H. Prescott and Ill. Robert C. Titus, were declared unanimously elected. Duration of the term of each was decided by lot, with the following result: Ill. Robert C. Titus, one year; Ill. Francis G. Ward, two years and Ill. Joel H. Prescott, three years.

At a special meeting, held on Friday evening, December 8, 1905, announcement of the severe illness of Brother Charles E. Markham, Grand Secretary, was received with the most profound regret by the members, which found expression in a letter of commiseration and wishes of speedy and permanent recovery, from the brothers, accompanied by a beautiful floral offering. Ill. Joel H. Prescott, First Lieutenant-Commander was deputized to convey the testimonial in person to the indisposed Brother.

An incident of the meeting, having peculiar significance in connection with the illness of Brother Markham, was the presentation of Harry Dwight Hosmer, as a candidate for Consistory degrees and membership. Brother Hosmer had demitted to Palmoni Lodge of Perfection from Niagara Lodge, Niagara Falls. It was an unusual incident that he was acting as Secretary of the Lodge at the time his petition for affiliation was received and acted upon. Brother Hosmer, who had rendered valuable assistance to the Secretary in the clerical work of his office, was obligated in all the degrees from the 19th to the 32d inclusive. On this occasion, for the first time, the duties of

Acting Grand Secretary of the Consistory devolved upon him, duties which he performed with the same close attention to detail, and conscientious loyalty, as have characterized his work as the legitimate successor to the late Brother Markham, in all the later years. In the class of ten which on this evening were advanced to the degree of Grand Pontiff, we find the name of Edwin Bert Henshaw, who has proven one of the Consistory's loyal and efficient workers.

Fourth Triennial Meeting.

At the fourth triennial meeting of the Consistory, held on Friday evening, December 22, 1906, Ill. Robert C. Titus announced that the proposed articles of incorporation had been prepared pursuant to orders of the Consistory. The legal document, which was to assume far-reaching importance in the succeeding years, was received and ordered spread upon the minutes. The regular triennial election followed, at which all the elective officers were returned to their former stations, with the exception of Ill. George L. Brown, who was returned to his previous station as Minister of State, his place as Second Lieutenant-Commander being taken by Ill. William H. Lyons. Installation of officers was conducted by Ill. Robert C. Titus, 33° Active, representing the Supreme Council. Appointments made by the Commander-in-Chief were not announced until the succeeding meeting, at which time, Brother George H. Clarke, whose kindly face and pleasing personality have been a welcome light to the members at nearly every gathering of the Scottish Rite clan in the Valley of Buffalo, ever since, was appointed Grand Sentinel. One of the oldest, one of the most faithful, though heavily burdened with the weight of years, it is the hope of the writer that for years to come fate may preserve to us his genial, encouraging presence. At this meeting William Tomilson was appointed Assistant Grand Sentinel and Ulysses S. Thomas, Organist.

Fourteenth Annual Reunion.

The Fourteenth Annual Reunion was memorable from the fact that it was the first meeting held in the new Delaware Avenue quarters. During the year which had elapsed since taking over the former church property, the edifice had been internally transformed, at heavy expense and much labor. When it is considered that the cost of reconstruction has reached the enormous figure of $74,663.98, some realization of the extent of the changes wrought, may be obtained. But the guiding forces of the great organization held some conception of the expanding future and were building to meet the requirements of that future. How sound was their reasoning, the present and ever increasing magnitude of the enterprise must testify.

At this reunion, acting as the direct representative of the Supreme Council, Ill. Robert C. Titus, performed the impressive ceremony of inaugurating, consecrating and dedicating the Scottish Rite

Cathedral. He was assisted by Ill. John L. Brothers, as Grand Prelate and a number of visiting 33d degree Masons. Following the dedication ceremonies, the 32d degree, Sublime Prince of the Royal Secret, was conferred upon a class of 125, in ceremonial form.

In this class were many brothers who have since proven their zeal for the order and their appreciation of the honor conferred, by joining the ranks of the workers, not all, perhaps, in the front rank as carriers of heavy parts, but one as essential as the other, in rounding out and bringing to perfection the beautiful work of the order. In this list was included Byron B. Daggett, later to become Sovereign Prince of Palmoni Council. At this reunion the 19th, 20th, 21st, 25th, 27th, 29th and 32d degrees were conferred in full form and ceremony.

Distinguished Guests.

Among the 33d degree Brothers in attendance from abroad were Ill. John B. Ellis, Most Puissant Grand Commander of the Supreme Council of Canada; Ill. Edwin D. Washburn, Past Commander-in-Chief of Aurora Gratta Consistory, Brooklyn, N. Y.; Ill. Robert H. Weems, Past Most Wise and Perfect Master of Aurora Gratta Chapter of Rose Croix, Brooklyn; Ill. William Ogden Campbell, Past Thrice Potent Master Aurora Gratta Lodge of Perfection, Brooklyn; Ill. Robert B. Sears and Ill. Thomas F. Watson, Jersey City; Ill. William F. Robie, Richmond, Ind.; Ill. William

W. Austach, Williamsport, Pa.; Ill. William E. Jewett, Adrian, Mich. Jewels and rings of the 33d degree were presented to Ill. George Clinton and Ill. Sheldon S. Broadhead, by the Commander-in-Chief. Prince Percy S. Lansdowne, president of the class of 1906, presented Ill. Francis G. Ward with a handsome basket of flowers, in appreciation, by the members, of the beautiful work. The reunion closed with a banquet at the Iroquois Hotel, to which 470 members and guests sat down.

An incident of the evening was the presentation, by Brother Harry W. Crabbs, on behalf of Buffalo Chapter of Rose Croix, to Ill. John L. Brothers, a Past Most Wise and Perfect Master's jewel, in appreciation of the many years of valuable service he had given that body. Thus ended a truly memorable gathering of Scottish Rite Masons in the Valley of Buffalo, a reunion which was merely an earnest of the many important and successful gatherings of the craft in their now sumptuous home and meeting place, which have followed and which are still to come.

Broadening The Work.

In its new and commodious Cathedral, Buffalo Consistory set out to broaden its work, to expand its social and fraternal possibilities and to inspire the Masonic brothers of the district, with the desirability of alliance with the rapidly growing body. At the first meeting held after the summer vacation in 1906, the Commander-in-Chief, named several new committees, for the purpose of stimulating interest and providing a more perfect working organization. These included a membership, schedule, ritual and parts, refreshments and entertainment committees. The chairmen of these committees were: Brother Harry W. Crabbs, Ill. Francis G. Ward, Ill. William H. Lyons, and Ill. Joel H. Prescott, respectively. To the committee on ritual and parts there were also added as chairmen for their respective bodies, Harry W. Crabbs, for the Rose Croix Chapter, William H. Hotchkiss for Palmoni Council, and Martin H. Blecher for Palmoni Lodge. At this meeting, the term of Ill. Robert C. Titus as trustee having expired, he was unanimously re-elected.

At the regular meeting of February 22, 1907, George K. Staples for the first time presided at the exemplification in full form, of the 29th degree, Knight of St. Andrew. In the class to receive the degree that evening were Charles D. Bigelow, Louis H. Dietzer, William H. Ellis, Harry C. Elwood, Walter A. Fleming, and others, all of whom were later to become active participants in the work of the Consistory.

Fifteenth Annual Reunion.

Opening on February 3, 1907, the Fifteenth Annual Reunion gave renewed evidence of the increasing activity of the Consistory officers, and the results of well-applied effort on the part of the membership committee. The class to receive the highest degree conferred in the Consistory, numbered 135, in which were included nine clergymen. They were the Rev. Coleman E. Byram, the Rev. Franklin J. Estabrook, the Rev. Joseph K. Griffis, the Rev. Gordon E. Hendshaw, the Rev. McIlyar H. Lichliter, the Rev. Ward Beecher Pickard, the Rev. Allen C. Prescott, the Rev. William H. Schild, the Rev. John W. Stitt. William J. Gomph, who was later to become an important figure in the musical organization of the Body, was a member of the class of 1907. Following the conferring of the 32d degree upon the large class, Commander-in-Chief Francis G. Ward presented to each brother of the membership committee, a beautiful 32d degree collar, as an expression of the appreciation of the Consistory for excellent work accomplished. The Commander also presented to Harry W. Crabbs, Most Wise Master of Buffalo Chapter of Rose Croix, a past Most Wise Master's jewel, as a token of approval of the effective work done by Brother Crabbs in the Rose Croix Chapter. It was accompanied by an expression of sincere regret, that circumstances required the removal of the recipient from the City of Buffalo, and the loss of his valuable services by Buffalo Consistory. Ill. Charles F. Bishop was on this occasion made the recipient of a ring and jewel of the 33d degree.

First Flag Day Celebration.

On June 14th, 1907, was held the first public celebration by Buffalo Consistory of Flag Day. That the Consistory officials were actuated by a high principle of patriotism, in thus setting apart a day on which to pay homage to the flag of our country, is fully shown in the notice of the meeting sent to every member. Its sentiments are of a character to stimulate pride in the thought that to be numbered among the Brothers of the Consistory, is to be enrolled among the faithful adherents of the greatest and most liberal government, which has, or ever will exist. Every sentence carried the glow of patriotic fervor, every word was an appeal for the closest intimacy between fraternity and love of country. It ran as follows; starting with an obligation:

"I will be loyal to the government of my country and support and obey the laws of the same."

"To the A. A. S. R.—:

On the 14th Day of June, 1777, Congress enacted:—

"That the flag of the thirteen United States be thirteen stripes, alternate red and white; that the union be thirteen stars, white in a blue field, representing a new constellation.

" 'Old Glory' for one hundred and thirty years has withstood mighty tests.

"It has become the symbol of a mighty nation.

"It has been carried to the uttermost parts of the earth, carrying Liberty wherever it has been thrown to the breeze.

"Americans cannot fail of a feeling of pride and satisfaction, when we contrast the meaning in far distant lands, of ours and other flags displayed.

"Let us earnestly exhort our citizens to join in making 'Flag Day' an event, and its celebration in 1907 a *great* event.

FRED ERFLING, 32°
MEMBER OF FIRST CLASS IN BUFFALO CONSISTORY, WHICH
NUMBERED THREE, AND FIRST ORGANIST OF THAT
BODY AFTER ITS ORGANIZATION

"Let us fling the Stars and Stripes to the breeze on June 14, 1907.

"May it greet the rising and salute the setting sun, floating the day long from every church, school and building, public and private however humble, throughout the land."

The appeal was signed by Ill. Robert C. Titus, Ill. Francis G. Ward and Ill. Joel H. Prescott, Trustees; and by Martin H. Blecher, Thrice Potent Master of Palmoni Lodge of Perfection, Walter M. Zink, Sovereign Prince of Palmoni Council Princes of Jerusalem, William D. Cushman, Most Wise Master of Buffalo Chapter of Rose Croix, Ill. Francis G. Ward, Commander-in-Chief and Charles E. Markham, Secretary.

Members of the Consistory assembled at the Cathedral at 6 o'clock in the morning and marched to the Terrace, where the Stars and Stripes were flung to the breeze from the Liberty pole, with a brief program including a prayer by the Prior, appropriate music by the Fife and Drum Corps, the national salute and the singing of "America." This ceremony was repeated at the City Hall and at Lafayette Square. Thus established, the custom has maintained, the number of patriotic citizens who participate increasing year by year.

A FURTHER CEREMONY.

At 7:30 o'clock the same evening a further ceremony in observance of the day, was held in the Cathedral, the following program being carried out: Invocation, by the Rev. Frank B. Carleton;

Song, "The Star Spangled Banner," address, Thomas Penney; song, "America," prayer, the Rev. John Dysart; song, "Now the Day is Over"; benediction, the Rev. D. H. Muller. Following the exercises a collation was served in the refrectory.

Careful preparation for the evening's ceremony had been made, the audience room of the Cathedral being handsomely decorated with flowers and ferns, while over all floated the several flags which mark the establishment and development of the Republic. These flags today constitute a treasured possession of Buffalo Consistory, an object of pride to the officers and members and of interest and speculation as to their meaning on the part of every new visitor to the handsome audience room. These flags are eight in number and may be described in their regular relation in the line of progression as hung, as follows:

Consistory Flags.

The first flag of Colonial succession. A Revolutionary banner known as the "Pine Tree Flag," and flown to the breeze during the Revolutionary years 1707 to 1776. It has a blood-red field, with a white union in the upper left hand corner, carrying a green pine tree.

First flag to float over permanent settlements in America. "The King's Colors," a union between the Red Cross of St. George of England and the White Cross of Scotland under King James I, in 1606. This was the flag of the Mayflower in 1620.

First flag of the American republic. Adopted by American Congress in Philadelphia, June 14, 1777, with thirteen stripes alternate red and white, with a blue union carrying a circle of thirteen white stars, symbolizing the thirteen original colonies.

The flag of Cromwell and Charles II. This flag was not accepted by the united colonies in the new world and was the cause of much dissension about 1707.

First flag of American expansion. The United States Congress upon the admission of two more states to the American Union, added two more stars to the flag on July 1, 1795.

First flag to float over American soil. "Red Cross of St. George" the banner of Richard Coeur de Lion in 1192, and planted at Labrador by Sabastian Cabot in 1497, as the royal sign of Henry the Seventh. This flag is a wide blood-red cross upon a white field.

First flag of American Independence. Hoisted with a military salute of thirteen guns at Washington's headquarters in Cambridge, Massachusetts, January 2, 1776, and alluded to in "Old England," as "The Thirteen Rebellious Stripes." This flag is composed of thirteen red and white stripes—seven alternate on a white field, the union of blue carrying a Greek cross in white, supporting a Christian cross in red, the whole constituting thirteen stripes. There are no stars in this flag.

HISTORY OF BUFFALO CONSISTORY

A comprehensive and instructive history of our Consistory flag has been written by Ill. Charles W. Mann, 33°, custodian of the Consistory, which is a valuable addition to the Consistory literature.

Sixteenth Annual Reunion.

Another large class was in readiness for advancement on the occasion of the Sixteenth Annual Reunion which opened on April 22, 1908. It numbered 131, among whom were a number of brothers who have since been more or less active in degree work of the Consistory and in other Masonic bodies. At the sixteenth reunion more degrees were exemplified in full form than at any previous annual meeting. These and the officers presiding were as follows:

Nineteenth, Grand Pontiff, Prince Charles Elbert Rhodes presiding.

Twentieth, Master Ad Vitam, Prince Charles W. Mann presiding in first section; Ill. Francis G. Ward in second section.

Twenty-first, Patriarch Noachite, Ill. John L. Brothers presiding.

Twenty-fifth, Knight of the Brazen Serpent, Prince Howard D. Herr presiding.

Twenty-seventh, Commander of the Temple, Prince Otto W. Volger presiding in first section; Prince John Dysart presiding in second section; Ill. William H. Lyons as Frederick II.

Twenty-ninth, Knight of St. Andrew, Prince George K. Staples presiding.

ANCIENT ACCEPTED SCOTTISH RITE

Thirtieth, Knight Kadosh or Knight of the Black and White Eagle, Prince Herbert P. Bissell presiding.

Thirty-first, Grand Inspector Inquisitor Commander, Prince Percy S. Lansdowne presiding.

Thirty-second, Sublime Prince of the Royal Secret, Ill. Francis G. Ward presiding.

DECORATIONS PRESENTED.

At the close of the reunion, the Commander-in-Chief presented the Ill. Brothers, Alan H. G. Hardwicke and Ill. Charles E. Markham with the decorations of a Sovereign Grand Inspector General, Honorary, with the compliments of Buffalo Consistory. There was presented to the Consistory a framed portrait of the class of 1905, an example which has been followed by each succeeding class, thus preserving to the Consistory home, the faces of the dear brothers who are still among us, as well as those who have gone away from our fraternal circle, at the call of the Grand Architect of the Universe. As had long before become the established custom, there were present at this reunion, a large number of visiting Illustrious Brothers who had been honored by the Supreme Council.

At the regular meeting held on Friday evening, October 23, 1908, a delegation of officers and members of Moore Consistory, Hamilton, Ont., headed by Ill. Frederick J. Howell, 33°, Commander-in-Chief, paid a fraternal visit to Buffalo Consistory. For their entertainment, the Nineteenth degree was conferred in full form upon a class of six candidates, Prince Charles Elbert Rhodes presiding.

Seventeenth Annual Reunion.

Like its immediate predecessors, the Seventeenth Annual Reunion was marked by the introduction of a large class of candidates, indicating that the Consistory membership growth was to be permanent and substantial. There were 117 loyal Masons to receive the 32d degree. At this reunion three degrees, which had not before been exemplified in full form in Buffalo Consistory, were put on, adding immeasurably to the interest of the meeting. These degrees and the brothers presiding were: Twenty-second, Prince of Libanus, Ill. Martin H. Blecher; Twenty-third, Chief of the Tabernacle, Prince Edward D. Peters; Twenty-fourth, Prince of the Tabernacle, Prince Charles W. Mann.

On this occasion, Ill. William Homan, 33° Active, Deputy of the Supreme Council for New York, was a visitor for the first time. Another distinguished guest of the Consistory was Ill. William Gibson, active member of the Supreme Council of Canada. Both the distinguished visitors were presented by the Commander-in-Chief and addressed the large number of Princes assembled, in eloquent and eulogistic terms. Certificates of honorary membership and the accompanying jewels were presented by Commander-in-Chief Ward, to Ill. William Homan, Ill. William Gibson, Ill. George Henry Kenyon and Brother Judson C. McKenzie.

ANCIENT ACCEPTED SCOTTISH RITE

Ill. Martin Blecher, chairman of the membership committee, also presented handsome Consistory caps on behalf of the Body, to those members who had presented the applications of two or more candidates for admission. The recipients were: Princes Charles H. Andrews, John D. Campbell, Ole E. Goldhagen, George A. Halbin, Sylvanus B. Nye, William J. Paya, Henry J. Zilch, Bernard Cohen, John P. Diehl, Jr., Walter F. Gibson, Louis G. Hayward, Joseph H. Nichols, George W. Poole, Albert H. Zink, James B. Cloudsley, Walter A. Fleming, Charles I. Heckman, Charles W. Mann, James L. Nixon, Lloyd L. Westbrook.

Acting on request of the Commander-in-Chief, Ill. William Homan presented on behalf of the Consistory to Ill. Morris Benson, the decoration and ring of a Sovereign Grand Inspector General, Honorary, and Ill. Francis G. Ward deputized Ill. Martin H. Blecher to convey to Ill. William L. Alexander, a similar decoration and ring.

FIFTH TRIENNIAL MEETING.

At the Fifth Triennial Session of Buffalo Consistory, held on Friday evening, May 28, 1909, a communication under date of April 20, 1909, signed by Ill. Samuel C. Lawrence, Sovereign Grand Commander, announcing the resignation of Ill. Henry L. Palmer, and his succession to the office of Sovereign Grand Commander, was received. On motion of Ill. Joel H. Prescott, the Secretary was directed to forward to the new Sovereign Grand Commander, at Boston, Mass., an expression of the allegiance of Buffalo Consistory to the new chief officer of the Rite, the unanimous expression of the members being manifested by a rising vote.

At the election of officers which followed, all the incumbents were returned unanimously to their respective stations. New appointments of the Commander-in-Chief were: Rt. Rev. Joseph F. Berry, Prior; George J. Metzger, Engineer and Seneschal; Martin H. Blecher, Standard Bearer; William F. Elmendorf, Guard; P. Frederick Piper, Historian; William J. Gomph, Organist. The officers elected and appointed, with the exception of the Commander-in-Chief, were then installed by Ill. Francis G. Ward, assisted by Ill. Otto W. Volger, as Grand Marshal, representing the Supreme Council.

There was also received at this meeting notice of the death of Ill. Henry L. Palmer, who had passed away from life's activities on May 6, 1909, less than a month after his resignation as Sovereign Grand Commander. Action taken at a regular meeting of Palmoni Council Princes of Jerusalem, conferring honorary membership in the four Buffalo Scottish Rite bodies, upon Ill. Edwin D. Washburn of Brooklyn; Ill. Arthur MacArthur, Troy, N. Y., and Ill. James H. Codding, Grand Secretary General of the Supreme Council, whose home was in Towanda, Pa., was unanimously approved.

HARRY D. HOSMER, 32°
SECRETARY OF ALL THE BODIES OF THE SCOTTISH RITE IN THE
VALLEY OF BUFFALO AND ORGANIZER AND DIRECTOR
OF THE ENTERTAINERS

ANCIENT ACCEPTED SCOTTISH RITE

Celebration of Whitsunday.

On May 13, 1909, was held the first celebration, with impressive ceremonies by Buffalo Consistory, of Whitsunday. From the elaborate notice of this meeting sent to the members, we learn that there had died during the six years between 1903 and 1909, forty-one members. Exercises opened with a processional, in which were represented the officers of all the Accepted Scottish Rite bodies of the Valley of Buffalo, Charter Members of Buffalo Consistory and the Class of 1909. Those participating in the impressive ceremonies were the Rev. John Dysart, the Rev. Frank B. Carleton, the Rev. Thomas French, Ill. Horace A. Noble, the Rev. G. Sherman Burrows, the Rev. Joseph F. Berry. The singers were as follows: Sopranos, Mrs. Walter B. Hawke, Mrs. Talbot Howe. Altos, Mrs. Henry House Griffin, Mrs. Laura D. Minehan. Tenors, Charles E. Mott, William Slaight, Dr. Prescott LeBreton. Bases, Fred G. Roginson, Edward Tanner, William B. Todd, H. B. Hodges, with William G. Gomph as Organist and Director. There was a large attendance of members and visitors. The following tribute to the spirit prompting the day's observance, written by a devoted member of the craft, appeared on the printed program. It is reproduced, as indicating the underlying principles of a great order; the touching relationship between our own noble profession and the Christian Church. It was as follows:

"Masonry is not of itself a religion. Every good Mason respects the religion of his brother, though differing perhaps from his own, and hopes that all may be true in those respects where differences arise, and that each may be sufficiently near to Truth to solve for himself the great problem of Life and Death. Surely, no one who has looked thoughtfully on the checkered road through the wilderness of life, or who has stood even for a moment near the brink of the cold river of Death, would be otherwise than reverential in the presence of any shrine to which a fellow creature may kneel for aid or consolation."

Suitable observance of Whitsunday has been a never neglected duty of Buffalo Consistory, since the above mentioned occasion.

Eighteenth Annual Reunion.

The Eighteenth Annual Reunion convened on Tuesday afternoon, March 29, 1910. The class numbered 105 members. Certificates of honorary membership in the Buffalo Bodies were presented to Ill. Arthur MacArthur, 33°, Ill. Edwin D. Washburn, 33° and Ill. James H. Codding, 33°. On behalf of the Consistory, Ill. Francis G. Ward also presented to Ill. Martin H. Blecher and Ill. George Fobes the grand decoration and ring of a Sovereign Grand Inspector General, Honorary. Prince George K. Staples in behalf of the class of 1908, presented to the Consistory a handsome piece of furniture for the foyer, a framed picture of the class and a class banner.

At the regular rendezvous held on Friday evening, January 27, 1911, Ill. Martin H. Blecher presided in the absence of the Commander-in-Chief. A most painful duty devolved upon the presiding officer at this time, it being that of announcing to the members the sad news of the death of two brothers, whose loyalty to the Consistory and admirable services through a period of years, had made them conspicuous figures in the fraternity. They were Ill. Charles E. Markham, 33°, Grand Secretary, and Ill. Horace A. Noble, 33°. Ill. Brother Markham passed away on January 24, and Ill. Brother Noble on January 27, only three days later. Owing to absence of the Commander-in-Chief, appropriate action relative to the great loss the Consistory had sustained, was deferred until a subsequent meeting.

On the date of Illustrious Brother Markham's death, Harry D. Hosmer, who had been the efficient Acting Secretary, was appointed by the Commander-in-Chief to fill the vacancy thus caused; the appointment being ratified later by the Consistory.

Nineteenth Annual Reunion.

The Nineteenth Annual Reunion opened with an executive session on Tuesday afternoon, April 11, 1911. At the succeeding sessions, all the degrees from the 19th to the 32d inclusive, were conferred in full form and ceremony, with the exception of the 26th and 28th. The class was large, containing 155 candidates. There were present on this occasion, the following honorary or active members of the Supreme Council: Ill. William Homan, Deputy for New York; Ill. Judson C. McKenzie, Fall River, Mass.; Ill. George F. Sinclair, Grand Rapids, Mich.; Ill. George W. Fuller, and Ill. Hugh H. Kendall, Corning, N. Y. All briefly addressed the Consistory when introduced by the Commander-in-Chief. Ill. Francis G. Ward presented a certificate of honorary membership in the Buffalo Bodies to Ill. John Comosh, of Corning, and a similar testimonial was directed to be sent to Ill. John Lloyd Thomas in New York. The Commander-in-Chief, on behalf of Buffalo Consistory, also invested Ill. Joseph H. Horton with the decoration and ring of a Sovereign Grand Inspector General. Probably no similar preferment has been received by the membership of the Consistory with more sweeping evidences of approval. On behalf of the friends of Ill. Brother Horton, he was presented by Ill. Judson McKenzie, with a handsome bouquet of roses. Remarks of both the presentor and recipient were most touching in their expressions of fraternal brotherhood and good-will. A banquet closed the reunion.

At the regular rendezvous of Buffalo Consistory, held on January 26, 1912, Prince George K. Staples, representing Ill. Francis G. Ward as Commander-in-Chief, presided. The session was marked by the attendance as a welcome guest, of Ill. John Lloyd Thomas, Commander-in-Chief of New York City Consistory. The 25th degree, Knight of the Brazen Serpent, was conferred upon a class of 80.

ANCIENT ACCEPTED SCOTTISH RITE

Twentieth Annual Reunion.

The Twentieth Annual Reunion which convened on April 9, 1912, apparently marked a new epoch in the history of Buffalo Consistory, for it reflected stronger interest and more substantial results, than any which had preceded it. A class of 245 candidates were instructed in the higher mysteries of the Craft. This stimulation of interest was doubtless due, largely, to the character of the officers of all the subordinate bodies, who had been working hard to improve the quality and amount of ritualistic work displayed in their respective organizations. Among these enthusiastic and capable officers, whose efforts had been loyally supported by their subordinates and lay members, were George K. Staples, Walter M. Zink, Albert H. Zink, William H. Ellis, Martin H. Blecher, Otto W. Volger, Hugh A. Sloan, Harry W. Crabbs, Fred B. Griffith, Jr., and Charles H. Andrews. These energetic officers had wrought with ever increasing zeal in behalf of their beloved Consistory, and results, though not so strongly marked at first, were beginning to tell in generous measure. Beyond this was an interested membership, now reaching well to the two thousand mark, and the influence of these, extending through and from those already honored by advancement to the high degrees, was having its influence upon their brothers, as yet without the charmed circle. After its years of struggle, of personal sacrifices of officers and members of time and effort, in opposition to adverse sentiment and unjust criticism, Buffalo Consistory had kept itself particularly free from internal misunderstandings and differences, and was finally coming into its own.

At this reunion there was, as usual, a large number of visiting 33d degree Brothers in attendance. The session lasted for four days and every hour of available time was occupied with the exemplification in full form of the beautiful degree work. At the close, Ill. Francis G. Ward presented to Ill. Joseph F. Berry the grand decoration and ring of the 33d degree. Similar distinction had fallen upon William D. Cushman, and the secretary was directed to forward to him in New York, the insignia of his advancement. Certificates of honorary membership in the Buffalo Body were issued to Ill. Frederick J. Howell and Ill. Jay B. Kline.

A pleasing feature marked the closing session, it being the presentation, by the Commander-in-Chief, in behalf of the members, to Past Sovereign Princes of Palmoni Council, Walter M. Zink and Albert H. Zink, Past Sovereign Prince jewels. Never was reward of merit more appropriately bestowed. Never was appreciation more clearly displayed than in the subsequent loyalty and unselfish zeal for the welfare of the several bodies, displayed by these two earnest, devoted Brothers.

Sixth Triennial Meeting.

At the sixth triennial election held on May 24, 1912, fourteen Illustrious members of the Supreme Council from the jurisdiction of Buffalo Consistory, Active or Honorary, were in attendance. They were as follows: William L. Alexander, Morris Benson, Martin H. Blecher, Sheldon B. Broadhead, George L. Brown, George Fobes, Walter D. Greene, Alan H. G. Hardwicke, Frank B. Hower, William H. Lyons, Joel H. Prescott, Samuel Root, Robert C. Titus, Francis G. Ward. These were a portion of those brothers who by virtue of exceptional work for the Rite, had won deserved promotion to the most exalted degree.

At this meeting was received a proposition from the executors of the Blocher estate, outlining the terms and conditions under which the Scottish Rite Bodies of the Valley of Buffalo could purchase the Blocher property in Delaware Avenue, adjoining the Scottish Rite Cathedral. This proposition had already been received in Palmoni Lodge of Perfection and was referred to the Consistory for consideration. After prolonged discussion, a vote of expression was taken resulting in favor of the proposition, final action to be taken at the meeting on June 7. A letter was read from Brother S. M. Logan of Moore Consistory, Hamilton, Ont., expressing appreciation for the honor conferred upon Ill. Commander-in-Chief F. J. Howell, of Moore Consistory, in electing him to honorary membership in Buffalo Consistory.

In the election which followed, a decided change was marked in the selection of officers. The result was as follows: George K. Staples, Commander-in-Chief; Walter D. Greene, First Lieutenant-

HISTORY OF BUFFALO CONSISTORY

A Progressive Policy.

Commander; Harry L. Taylor, Second Lieutenant-Commander; William F. Elmendorf, Orator; Walter M. Zink, Chancellor; Samuel Root, Treasurer; Harry D. Hosmer, Secretary; Robert C. Titus, Trustee for three years, Francis G. Ward, Trustee for two years, George K. Staples, Trustee for one year.

In the appointments by the newly elected Commander-in-Chief which followed, was indicated the progressive policy to be adopted by the new head of the large fraternal body. In addition to the regular subordinate officers of the Consistory, which were not altered in personnel, an executive staff was named composed of the following: George J. Metzger, Director of Stage; Harry D. Hosmer, Assistant Director of Stage; Carl W. Knaus, Master of Properties; Arthur F. Isham, Assistant Master of Properties; William P. Mashinter, Electrician; Charles W. Mann, Master of Wardrobe; Henry Haier, Assistant Master of Wardrobe; William D. Camp, Assistant Secretary (later to be succeeded by Frederick B. Griffith, Jr., who still serves with zeal and efficiency); William J. Flierl, Class Conductor; Henry B. Saunders, Chairman of Publicity Committee. The officers elected and appointed were duly installed by Ill. Francis G. Ward, assisted by Ill. George L. Brown as Marshal, William F. Elmendorf as Captain of the Guard and John S. Embleton as Sentinel, representing the Supreme Council. On behalf of Buffalo Consistory, Commander-in-Chief George K. Staples presented Ill. Brother Francis G. Ward with a Past Commander-in-Chief's jewel, which was received with generous expression of appreciation.

At the meeting of November 29, 1912, a class of 116 were recipients of the Nineteenth degree, conferred upon them in full form. At this meeting, Ill. Francis T. Coppins was presented with a 33° jewel by the class of that year, of which he was a member. The presentation was made by Ill. Walter D. Greene.

Reception to Bishop Burt.

A special rendezvous of Buffalo Consistory was held on January 18, 1913, in conjunction with the other Scotish Rite bodies of the Valley of Buffalo, for the purpose of welcoming, receiving and introducing Bishop William Burt, of the Methodist Episcopal Church, a 32d degree member under the jurisdiction of the Supreme Council of Italy, Bishop Burt having for many years been a missionary in that country. Officers of the various bodies were presented and welcomed by Commander-in-Chief Staples and his Lieutenants, Ill. Walter D. Greene and Brother Harry L. Taylor. Ceremonies of the evening were opened in due form, with prayer by Ill. Francis T. Coppins and the singing of "America." Bishop Burt was introduced by Brother Charles W. Mann, and presented by him to the Ill. Commander-in-Chief. A most cordial fraternal greeting was extended by the Ill.

Commander-in-Chief to the guest of honor, who was then in turn formally introduced to the Consistory members. The Bishop voiced his great pleasure at the reception accorded him, and at the opportunity thus afforded to meet and greet the brethren of the Scottish Rite in Buffalo.

In his address which followed, he gave a most interesting description of his life as a Mason in Italy, and explained the progress being made by the Craft beyond the seas. He also spoke instructively of Italy's progress and development, predicting a bright future for the kingdom, under changing and improving conditions. After a solo by Mrs. Griffin, a formal reception was held, at which all members of the Consistory were given opportunity to grasp the hand of the visiting brother and to express their appreciation of his presence. With the singing of "Old Hundred," the meeting was dismissed.

Twenty-first Annual Reunion.

At the Twenty-first Annual Reunion, the first under direction of Ill. George K. Staples, five days were required for the session, opening on Monday evening, March 24th, and closing on the 28th. The class numbered 303. All the Consistory degrees, with the exception of the 26th and 28th, were conferred in full form. Honorary membership jewels were presented to Ill. Hugh H. Kendall and Ill. George W. Fuller of Corning, who were among the Supreme Council members in attendance. Ill.

George K. Staples also presented to Brother Abram Oppenheimer and Brother George L. Kingston, Past Thrice Potent Masters of Palmoni Lodge of Perfection, appropriate jewels. The grand decoration of the 33d degree was also presented by Ill. Brother Staples to Ill. Francis T. Coppins, and Ill. Robert C. Titus, on behalf of the Consistory, presented a similar decoration to Ill. George K. Staples.

On June 27th, 1913, a new departure in the Consistory program was inaugurated. Up to this time no meetings had been held following the annual election and installation of officers, in May, until after the summer vacation. Ill. Commander-in-Chief Staples, doubtless reflecting that continued interest was likely to prove beneficial to the Consistory and its membership, had determined to hold mid-summer meetings, to receive petitions and confer degrees. At meetings held on June 26th and 27th, petitions were received from 78 Knights of the Rose Croix, and they were duly advanced to the 32d degree, the 21st and 24th degrees being conferred in full form. On motion of Ill. George K. Staples, Commander-in-Chief, honorary membership was conferred upon Ill. Harry J. Guthrie, Deputy of Delaware. A complete set of the Flags of our Country were then presented on behalf of Buffalo Consistory, to Ill. William Homan, 33°, Active, Deputy for New York and Commander-in-Chief of the Council of Deliberation, for the State of New York. This ended the sessions of the Consistory, for that year, until October, when work was resumed with renewed interest.

Thanksgiving Observance.

On Thursday afternoon, November 27, 1913, was held the first public Thanksgiving Day exercises by Buffalo Consistory. A pleasing and devout program was carried out by the members of the four bodies. Masons, with their families and friends, were invited to be present. There was a large attendance. A historical address by the Commander-in-Chief, was a feature. It was supplemented by the following poem of Thanksgiving, written by Ill. George K. Staples:

> All the plenty Summer pours;
> Autumn's rich, o'erflowing stores;
> Flocks that whiten all the plain;
> Yellow sheaves or ripened grain;
> Lord, for these our souls shall raise
> Grateful vows and solemn praise.
>
> As thy prospering hand hath blessed,
> May we give Thee of our best;
> And by deeds of kindly love,
> For thy mercies grateful prove;
> Singing thus through all our days;
> "Praise to God, immortal praise."
>
> Bless, O God, the Scottish Rite;
> Give the brothers strength and light;
> Buffalo shall better be
> For its good Consistory
> Teaches men the truths of life;
> Live in peace and not in strife.
>
> As we leave this temple grand,
> Firmly grasp a brother's hand;
> Say a word of love and cheer;
> God is always very near.
> Thanks we give to God above
> For his gift of life and love.

ANCIENT ACCEPTED SCOTTISH RITE

TWENTY-SECOND REUNION.

Although the class of 1914 was not so large at the time of the annual reunion, the Twenty-second, as in the previous year, it was of substantial size, numbering 284. Added to these the 78 advanced at the June meeting of 1913, and which must of necessity be included in the class of 1914, we find that the net result of the year's effort was 362, a most satisfactory record. The Twenty-second reunion was marked by no unusual features.

On May 22, 1914, a meeting was held at which it was announced that it had been called for the purpose of installing the officers of Palmoni Lodge of Perfection, Palmoni Council Princes of Jerusalem and Buffalo Chapter of Rose Croix. The officers elected and appointed were accordingly installed, by Ill. George K. Staples, Commander-in-Chief, assisted by Ill. Charles W. Mann as Marshal.

Following the plan adopted in the previous year, a business meeting of Buffalo Consistory was held on May 28th, following that at which officers were installed, and petitions received. Forty petitioners were presented and received the 19th and 26th degrees, the same being conferred upon them in full form and ceremony. At this time the 26th degree, Prince of Mercy, was for the first time presented in full form in Buffalo Consistory, Brother Charles I. Heckman, Deputy Master of Palmoni Lodge, presiding at the exemplification of the degree. On the succeeding Friday evening, May

29th, the 32d degree, Prince of the Royal Secret, was conferred upon the members of this class, First Lieutenant-Commander Ill. Walter D. Greene presiding.

Twenty-third Annual Reunion.

At the annual reunion in 1915, there was a class of 250 and the sessions were marked by large attendance and sustained interest among the degree workers and visitors. The social features of the occasion were not overlooked by the energetic Commander-in-Chief and his efficient committees, and the brethren looked forward with increased confidence to the future.

A feature of the reunion of 1915, was the attendance of thirty-one Thirty-third degree Masons, members of the Committee on Charitable Foundation. At the head was Most Puissant Barton Smith, 33°, of Toledo, O., ex-officio chairman of the committee. Meetings in connection with the business of the Committee were held in the Hotel Iroquois, but the members were visitors to the Consistory, and guests of the Buffalo Scottish Riters, during their stay in Buffalo. They were enthusiastic in their commendation of the work of the reunion and expressed, in no measured terms, their pleasure at the wonderful development of Buffalo Consistory and co-ordinate bodies. Members of the Committee in attendance at the reunion were:

M. P. Barton Smith, 33°, Toledo, O.; Ill. Albro Elmore Chase, 33°, Portland, Me.; Ill. Charles F. Johnson, 33°, Waterville, Me.; Ill. George W. Currier, 33°, Nashua, N. H.; Ill. George I. McAllister, 33°, Manchester, N. H.; Ill. Marsh Olin Perkins, 33°, Windsor, Vt.; Ill. Kittredge Haskins, 33°, Brattleboro, Vt.; Ill. Arthur G. Polard, 33°, Lowell, Mass.; Ill. John L. Bates, 33°, Boston, Mass.; Ill. Charles C. Mumford, 33°, Ill. George H. Holmes, 33°, Providence, R. I.; Ill. Charles L. Hubbard, 33°, Ill. John C. Averill, 33°, Norwich, Conn.; Ill. John Lloyd Thomas, 33°, Ill. James H. Codding, 33°, New York City; Ill. Robert F. Sherrifs, 33°, Ill. William D. Wolfskiel, 33°, Elizabeth, N. J.; Ill. George W. Kendrick, 33°, Philadelphia, Pa.; Ill. David A. Sawdey, 33°, Erie, Pa.; Ill. Harry Jones Guthrie, 33°, Ill. George M. Fisher, 33°, Wilmington, Del.; Ill. Frank Sheldon Harmon, 33°, Cleveland, O.; Ill. Charles J. Pretsman, 33°, Columbus, O.; Ill. John J. Carton, 33°, Flint, Mich.; Ill. Frank T. Lodge, 33°, Detroit, Mich.; Ill. William Geake, 33°, Fort Wayne, Ind.; Ill. Truman F. Palmer, 33°, Monticello, Ind.; Ill. Leroy A. Goddard, 33°, Chicago, Ill.; Ill. Lawrence V. Sherman, 33°, Springfield, Ill.; Ill. William W. Perry, 33°, Ill. Andrew D. Agnew, 33°, Milwaukee, Wis.

Visitors from Rochester.

At this Reunion, members of Rochester Consistory were present as guests of the Buffalo Bodies, and on Wednesday afternoon, April 28th, the Rochester Brethren conferred the 29th degree, Knight of St. Andrew, upon the members of the class, in full form. On that evening, the Buffalo

Consistory entertainers gave a special program by the Guido Chorus, for the pleasure of the large number of visitors. Another feature of the Twenty-third Annual Reunion was the attendance of members of Moore Consistory of Hamilton, Ont., who worked the 20th degree, Master Ad Vitum, in full form, winning high compliment for their presentation of the beautiful and impressive lesson.

Buffalo Consistory had at the time of this reunion, one Active and twenty-eight Honorary Members of the Supreme Council, as follows: Ill. Robert C. Titus, 33°, Active; William L. Alexander, Morris Benson, Martin H. Blecher, Shelden B. Broadhead, John L. Brothers, George L. Brown, George H. Clarke, George Clinton, Francis T. Coppins, William D. Cushman, William H. Ellis, George Fobes, Walter D. Greene, Alan H. G. Hardwicke, Edward W. Hatch, Charles E. Hayes, Howard D. Herr, Joseph H. Horton, Frank B. Hower, William H. Lyons, Charles W. Mann, Joel H. Prescott, Samuel Root, George K. Staples, Otto W. Volger, Francis G. Ward and George H. Woolley, Honorary.

Seventh Triennial.

At the triennial election which took place on May 28, the following officers were elected by unanimous vote of the members, the attendance being unusually large.

ILL. GEORGE K. STAPLES, 33°
COMMANDER-IN-CHIEF OF BUFFALO CONSISTORY, WHOSE EARNEST
AMBITIONS FOR THAT BODY, HAVE BEEN
ENCOURAGINGLY REALIZED

ANCIENT ACCEPTED SCOTTISH RITE

Ill. George K. Staples	*Commander-in-Chief*
Ill. Walter D. Greene	*First Lieut.-Commander*
Ill. William H. Ellis	*Second Lieut.-Commander*
Ill. Alan H. G. Hardwicke	*Orator*
Walter M. Zink	*Chancellor*
Ill. Samuel Root	*Treasurer*
Harry D. Hosmer	*Secretary*
Hugh A. Sloan	*Prior*
John S. Embleton	*Master of Ceremonies*
Andrew Shiels	*Hospitaler*
George J. Metzger	*Engineer and Architect*
Fred B. Griffith, Jr.	*Standard Bearer*
Fred M. Ackerson	*Guard*
Ill. Charles W. Mann	*Historian*
Ill. George H. Clarke	*Sentinel*
George L. Tucker	*Assistant Sentinel*

The brothers composing the staff are not only well qualified for their respective duties, but each has won the right to such preferment by meritorious work for the craft in the lower bodies. The Commander-in-Chief made the following special assignments:

George J. Metzger	*Director of Stage*
Harry D. Hosmer	*Assistant Director of Stage*
Carl W. Knaus	*Aide to Commander-in-Chief and Master of Properties*
Arthur F. Isham	*Assistant Master of Properties*
John M. Winship	*Stage Assistant*
William P. Mashinter	*Electrician*
Truman L. Ray	*Assistant Electrician*
Ill. Charles W. Mann	*Master of Wardrobe and Custodian of Consistory*
Harry Haier	*Assistant Master of Wardrobe*
Fred B. Griffith, Jr.	*Assistant Secretary*
Walter E. Schaefer	*Assistant Secretary*
William J. Flierl	*Marshal of Class*
Jacob Harris	*Registrar*
George J. Haffa	*Chairman of House Committee*
Wellington Z. Jarden	*Steward*

John M. Gleisner	*Outer Guard*
Charles Elbert Rhodes	*Literary Critic*
Carl Winnig	*Director of Chorus*
John W. Bolton	*Director of Band*

Much interest attached to this election, and its result was awaited with considerable interest, not only by the Buffalo brethren, but by those of sister jurisdictions, as was evinced by the hearty telegram received from Rochester Consistory, later in the evening, extending the congratulations of the Rochester Princes to Ill. George K. Staples on his unanimous re-election. Installation services were conducted by Ill. Charles W. Mann.

That the Masonic tide is setting strongly toward the Scottish Rite bodies in the Valley of Buffalo, is shown by the fact that on June 4, a class numbering 32 was presented, and on June 25 was advanced to the 32d degree. Again on October 22 there was a class of 40, which was increased to 111 who were made Princes of the Royal Secret, at the midwinter reunion in December. At the close of 1915 the total membership of the Consistory was 2,695. Eighteen members had died during the year, and ten had been lost by demit, but the net gain for the year was 238.

An Innovation.

On Thursday evening, June 26, 1913, the officers and members of Buffalo Consistory paid a fraternal visit to Charles W. Cushman Lodge, No. 879, F. & A. M., another innovation, it being the first visit of that character ever paid by a Scottish Rite body to a Blue Lodge. On this occasion Commander-in-Chief Staples presented to Cushman Lodge, through its Master, Edward G. Bodenbender, a handsome American flag, in the following words:

> Attention, Brothers, while we tell,
> How James L. Nixon did so well.
> He worked and strove and wrought and fought
> Till Cushman Lodge to life was brought.
> Its Master was he, at the start,
> He worked with zeal, with all his heart;
> With honors gained he did not shirk,
> Continued he to do some work.
> His work and life did us convince
> So made we him a Scottish Prince.
> Surprised you are to meet tonight,
> The brothers of the Scottish Rite,
> To Cushman Lodge we bring good cheer
> And nothing else does call us here.
> In token of our love most true,
> A flag we now present to you.
> Our banner waves on land and sea,
> An emblem of the people free.
> Uphold the flag of this our land,
> A loyal, true, devoted band
> Of Masons free and brothers brave,
> Prepared to fight, our land to save;
> Prepared to fight, though we may be,
> May peace and love and harmony
> Control our lives, direct our thoughts,
> Till sin and vice are brought to naught.

Such pleasing reference to Brother Nixon, was inspired by the fact that it was upon his initiative, that Cushman Lodge was organized, besides being for two and a half years at its beginning, Worshipful Master of the then baby Lodge of Buffalo. Brother Nixon was also an active member of Buffalo Consistory, of the class of 1908, and it was perhaps partially due to this fact, that the Scottish Rite visitors planned and carried out the innovation. Worshipful Master Bodenbender invited Ill. Commander Staples and Ill. William Homan, 33°

Active, Deputy for New York, who was with the visitors, to the East, and thanked the Consistory members for their visit and its purpose. Ill. Brother Homan spoke briefly of the unusual incident and expressed his belief that it was an augury of more close relations between the Blue Lodge and Scottish Rite. Brother Nixon thanked the visitors for the personal consideration shown and for the handsome gift.

PALMONI LODGE OF PERFECTION

Gateway to Consistory and First Scottish Rite Body in Buffalo.
Early Struggles and Final Success.

IN recording the progress of Buffalo Consistory, since its organization in 1893, we have, of necessity, traced to a considerable degree the career of the co-ordinate bodies of the Rite. It is through these alone, that admission to the higher grades can be obtained, and the success of the Consistory depends very largely upon the activity of the lower bodies. Palmoni Lodge of Perfection, and Palmoni Council, Princes of Jerusalem, were the initial Scottish Rite bodies in Buffalo, their organization occurring at the same time, though unfortunately no record of the Council previous to the fire of 1887 has been preserved. Palmoni Lodge, as the doorway to Scottish Rite Masonry in the Valley of Buffalo, has been the most important of the subordinate bodies, in its influence upon the development of Buffalo Consistory. In the Lodge the vital business of the great organization is transacted, and here the initiate receives his first instruction, catches his first glimpse of the beauties of the various grades.

Particularly interesting is the earliest available history of Palmoni Lodge, which, regardless of all obstacles presented, was prompted by an undaunted spirit of determined Masonic zeal, to press on to final success. Although the growth had been small, owing in some measure probably to the mistaken sentiment regarding Free Masonry created by the Morgan episode; the antagonism of members of the Egyptian rite, the slanders circulated by enemies of the craft, and the friendly but spirited rivalry of the York Rite, the misfortunes which overtook them, served apparently only to stimulate the leaders to renewed and more persistent effort, to place the Lodge on a substantial basis. Brother Pennell had been succeeded by James McCredie as Thrice Potent Master, and the latter by George M. Osgoodby. Their combined service extended over a period of fifteen years.

Scourged By Fire.

At the first regular communication following the fire in the Miller-Greiner building, in which all the records and lodge property had been destroyed, Palmoni Lodge convened in Ancient Landmarks rooms. The communication, which was held by dispensation on January 26, 1883, was attended by twenty-one brothers, including the officers, as follows:

G. M. Osgoodby	*Thrice Potent Master*
John C. Graves	*Deputy Master*
W. A. Woodsen	*Senior Warden*
Horace A. Noble	*Junior Warden*
S. M. Every	*Secretary*
J. M. McCredie	*Treasurer*
J. W. Tifft	*Master of Ceremonies*
M. Thielen	*Guard*
G. H. Clarke	*Hospitaler*
O. G. Nichols	*Orator*
C. R. Dunning	*Tiler*

ANCIENT ACCEPTED SCOTTISH RITE

Brothers present were: E. S. Knapp, Jacob Stern, William Weick, H. Klein, William Prouty, J. A. Given, T. C. Burns, G. R. W. Wolfe, H. Smith 2d and F. S. Coit.

It was announced by the Master that reading of the minutes of the last stated communication would be dispensed with, as they had been destroyed in the Miller-Greiner block fire. Petitions were received from two candidates, Will N. McCredie and Theodore L. Wadsworth, upon which favorable action was taken. Brother Wadsworth later became Secretary of all the subordinate bodies and was the first Secretary elected to serve in that capacity in the Consistory, organized in 1893. A committee composed of Brothers John C. Graves, G. M. Osgoodby and C. R. Dunning was appointed "to ascertain what property of the lodge has been saved from the fire and also what may be necessary to procure, in order to confer the degrees of the Lodge." The degrees from the 4th to the 14th were communicated to the two candidates.

At the succeeding meeting, held in the Lodge rooms of The Ancient Landmarks, on March 23, 1883, a dispensation of the Supreme Council was received, empowering the Lodge to hold an election of officers on that evening and also authorizing regular and special communications in the new location. Petitions were received from five candidates. At the election which followed the regular business, the following were chosen:

A. Oppenheimer	*Thrice Potent Master*
M. W. Cole	*Deputy Master*
W. A. Woodsen	*Senior Warden*
H. Smith 2d	*Junior Warden*
S. M. Every	*Secretary*
James McCredie	*Treasurer*
J. W. Tifft	*Master of Ceremonies*
M. Thielen	*Guard*
John Briggs	*Hospitaler*
Horace A. Noble	*Orator*
C. R. Dunning	*Tiler*

Installation followed the same evening.

An Important Petition.

A communication of importance to the interests of Scottish Rite Masonry in the Valley of Buffalo, was that of April 27, 1883, for on this occasion the petition for degrees and membership was received from Charles W. Cushman, who was destined to become the head, as well as the chief organizer, of Buffalo Consistory, ten years later. Hospitality, as well as fraternity, appears to have actuated the brothers of Palmoni Lodge in the early days as it has ever since—as it does all the bodies of the Scottish Rite at present. At this meeting an order was drawn for $18.94 for supplies for a "banquet" held at a previous special communication.

At the communication held on May 25, 1883, the summer vacation extending from June 30th to September 1st, was declared, and a notice was served upon Ancient Landmarks Lodge, announcing the proposed relinquishment of the rooms after that date, negotiations having been completed with

COMMANDER-IN-CHIEF'S ROOM, CONSISTORY HOUSE

the Masonic Hall Association for lodge room accommodations. A committee composed of Brothers O. G. Nichols, James McCredie and H. Smith 2d was appointed, with power to procure such paraphernalia as should be necessary, properly to exemplify the degrees. A committee to draft by-laws for the Lodge was also appointed, Brothers Mark W. Cole, S. M. Every and W. A. Woodsen being named.

At the last meeting of the year previous to the summer "call off" the resignation of S. M. Every as Secretary was received and Theodore L. Wadsworth was appointed to fill vacancy thus caused. At the succeeding meeting, held on September 27, in Masonic Hall at Washington and North Division streets, Secretary Wadsworth entered upon his new duties, duties performed faithfully and well, as the neatly kept and comprehensive minutes of the various bodies, for many years following, testify. His service in that capacity covered a period of thirteen years, being regretfully relinquished only when failing health compelled.

New By-Laws Adopted.

Business of importance having a bearing upon the future of Palmoni Lodge of Perfection was transacted at the meeting of Oct. 25, 1883. At that time, the by-laws prepared by the committee, were read for the second time and adopted. The committee on paraphernalia reported that $90 had been expended for that purpose. This incident is mentioned, that a contrast may be drawn by the present army of members, between the facilities available for the work of exemplification in 1883, and those enjoyed in the Scottish Rite Cathedral today. A motion was adopted, providing that all dues owing the Lodge, previous to the fire, be cancelled, and that a new account be opened with the members, commencing with January 1, 1883.

Tuesday, November 13th of that year was a really red-letter day for Palmoni Lodge, for on this occasion an exemplification of a degree in full form was had for the first time after the disastrous fire. The degrees of Secret Master, Perfect Master, Knight Elect of Nine and Grand, Perfect, Elect and Sublime Master were put on, in presence of probably the largest audience of members and visitors, that had ever assembled at any communication of the Lodge. This included forty-six members and officers of Palmoni, twenty-five members of Rochester Lodge of Perfection headed by Ill. William H. Whiting, 33°, ten members, headed by Ill. John Hodge, 33°, of Lock City Lodge and two members from Suspension Bridge, Ont., visitors. Exemplification of the degrees was under direction of Ill. Wm. H. Whiting, and the various roles were assumed by other members of Rochester Consistory. A banquet in honor of the visitors followed the Lodge work.

On January 24, 1884, at a regular communication, exemplification in full form of the beautiful work of the order was undertaken by the Lodge, under the new conditions. The degree of Secret Master was given under direction of Brother A. Oppenheimer, assisted by members of his official staff. Brother Henry C. Springer was the candidate of the evening. From this time forward, exemplification of the work in various degrees, became a regular feature of the communications.

AFTER REORGANIZATION.

The first annual election after reorganization, was held on February 28, 1884, the principal officers being retained. The first observance of St. John's Day, December 27, 1884, was observed by Palmoni Lodge, by holding a special communication for work and business, a dispensation from the Supreme Council being secured for that purpose. The dispensation was signed by Ill. R. M. C. Graham, 33°, Active, deputy for New York. At this special communication, a letter was received from the Supreme Council, announcing the death of Ill. Elbridge Gerry Hamilton, 33°, Deputy for the state of Indiana. The Illustrious Brother had passed away at his home in La Porte, Indiana, on October 28th. Afternoon and evening sessions of the Lodge were held on this date, the degrees of Secret Master, Intimate Secretary, Knight Elect of Nine and Grand Elect Perfect and Sublime Mason, being conferred in full form. At the annual election held on January 22, 1885, the principal officers were returned to their several stations, and were installed at the succeeding communication, Ill. George M. Osgoodby, Past Thrice Potent

Master of Palmoni Lodge, acting as installing officer. He was rewarded by a rising vote of thanks from the members.

First Deceased Member.

The first page in the new minute book to be inscribed with the name of a deceased member, was dedicated to Brother John A. Lockwood, who was summoned to the Grand Lodge above on February 20, 1885.

At the regular annual election held on January 28, 1886, Brother Mark W. Cole was advanced to the station of Thrice Potent Master and the retiring Master, whose efforts in behalf of the Lodge had been untiring and accompanied by a fair measure of success, accepted the station of Grand Orator. At this meeting, closing the first three years of the Lodge's existence under its new organization, the Secretary presented a voluminous report, from which we extract the following interesting facts.

Growth Was Slow.

During the year 1883, there was held thirteen communications, eleven stated and two special, at which the average attendance was twenty-four. Initiates 30. In 1884, ten communications were held, nine stated and one special, with an average attendance of nineteen. Initiates, 6. Six of the eleven degrees had been conferred in full form. The record for 1885 was even more discouraging, for although twelve communications were held, the average attendance was only fifteen and the total number of initiates 5. These figures are given, for the purpose of showing how difficult was the task undertaken by the devoted men who were laboring for the advancement of the Rite in the Valley of Buffalo, and the amount of discouragement which they were forced to meet. There can be no doubt, however, that the earnest and determined efforts they were making, was the good seed scattered upon fertile ground, which was later to spring up into a bountiful harvest. The total membership on January 1, 1883 had been 68. During the three years forty-one had been initiated, one added by affiliation and five removed by death, leaving a total membership of 105. Total receipts during the three years were $2,011.67; expenditures, $1,181. Balance in treasury, $130.51.

The year 1886 was unmarked by special incident in Palmoni Lodge, beyond the announcement on June 24th, of the death in the city of Providence, R. I., of the Ill. Thomas Arthur Doyle, 33°, mayor of that city and an active member of the Supreme Council, also of the demise of Ill. Rufus W. Landon, 33°, at Niles, Mich. Ill. Brother Landon is said to have been the first Mason inducted into the mysteries of the Craft in the state of Michigan, west of the city of Detroit. He was an emeritus member of the Supreme Council. Appropriate action was taken by the lodge, in acknowledgement of these regretable communications.

At the stated communication held on January 27, 1887, the result of the annual election was peculiar from the fact that the Master of Ceremonies, George L. Kingston, was advanced to the station of Thrice Potent Master, the other officers each going forward a single station. Brother Henry Smith 2d, Deputy Master, had retired from active office. During the year which followed, only six communications of the lodge were held, and degrees were communicated at but one session, two initiates being received. This depression in the work cannot be taken as a weakening of interest, or effort, on the part of the officers, but as the natural result of fate's decree. On March 15th, of that year, the Lodge had suffered from another disastrous fire which had swept away its paraphernalia, and deprived it temporarily of a home, though fortunately its books and records were saved. A dispensation was obtained permitting the officers to hold meetings in the Austin Building at Franklin and Eagle streets, but without the means of putting on the work in full form, there was little encouragement for membership effort. At the meetings held in the balance of the year, plans for rejuvenation were perfected, and the brethren looked forward with "freedom, fervency and zeal," to the future.

At the election held on January 28, 1888, the officers were returned without change. They were duly installed by Brother M. W. Cole, Past Thrice Potent Master.

ANCIENT ACCEPTED SCOTTISH RITE

At a meeting held on May 26, 1888, announcement of the death of the Treasurer, Brother James McCredie, who had been active in Lodge and Council, was made by the Thrice Potent Master, and that the election of a successor would be held at the next stated communication. The secretary was also directed to communicate with the District Deputy, in regard to a duplicate charter. At the succeeding meeting, on June 23, 1888, Brother William Baker was elected and installed Treasurer.

OPPENHEIMER RECALLED.

At the annual election, held on January 26, 1889, Brother A. Oppenheimer was again called to the responsible position of Thrice Potent Master, and from this date must be recorded the real progress of Palmoni Lodge, though the activity of the officers during the preceding years, had paved the way to success. With Brother Oppenheimer's election, Henry Smith 2d., was returned to the office of Deputy Master and Horace A. Noble was restored to the position of Orator. The remaining officers were retained in their former positions.

Among the brothers who presented petitions for degrees and membership on March 29, 1889, was John L. Brothers, whose later prominence in Lodge, Council, Chapter and Consistory work, warrants this mention. On the same evening, in company with three other brothers, he was instructed in the 4th degree, or Secret Master, in full form.

Palmoni Lodge lost another of its loyal members, when death came to Brother William H. Baker, Treasurer. The visit of the grim messenger occurred on April 26th. Notice of a special election, to be held on June 22d, to fill vacancy in the office of Treasurer, was given. The Thrice Potent also announced that he had appointed, temporarily, Brother Samuel Root to the duties of the office. This appointment was unanimously ratified at an election held at the next stated meeting.

At the meeting held on February 22, 1890, two reports from the Secretary were received, the first covering the period from January 1, 1886, to March 25, 1888, and the other from March 28, 1888, to February 22, 1890. By the first it was shown that the membership during the two-year period had been increased by 13, but there had been seven deaths and one brother had demitted, thus leaving the total membership on March 24, 1888, 110. The other report was of a more encouraging nature, showing that during 1889 thirty-six initiates had been received. The Lodge had, during that period, lost four members by death, leaving the total membership on February 22, 1890, 142.

On June 28, 1890, at a stated communication of the Lodge, the petition of Brother Charles E. Markham for degrees and membership was received and referred to the regular committee. At the following meeting on September 27th, Brother

CHARLES I. HECKMAN, 32°
THRICE POTENT MASTER OF PALMONI LODGE OF PERFECTION;
AN EARNEST AND UNTIRING WORKER IN CONSISTORY
AND CO-ORDINATE BODIES

Markham was elected. In November of the same year, George L. Brown, since prominent as a Lodge and Consistory worker, was elected to membership. Both brothers received the 14th degree, of Grand Elect Perfect and Sublime Mason, on December 29th, in a class with seventeen other candidates, one of whom was Ole E. Goldhagen, whose absence from any meeting of the Scottish Rite bodies today, would be noted.

CHANGE OF OFFICERS.

At the annual election of January 24, 1891, a clean sweep of the old officers, with the exception of Treasurer and Secretary, was made, with the following results: Charles W. Cushman, Thrice Potent Master; Charles A. DeLaney, Deputy Master; Orin G. Nichols, Senior Warden; Will H. Dick, Junior Warden; John L. Brothers, Orator. From the Secretary's report, presented at this meeting, it is noted that during the year, twenty-nine members had been added by initiation and one reinstated. There had been a loss of three by death and two by demit, making the total membership, on February 28, 1891, 167.

With the close of 1891 drawing near, arrangements were made for removal from the Austin Building to the new Masonic Temple in Niagara street, now approaching completion. At a meeting held on November 28th, the officers were empowered to make necessary arrangements for removal, including the procuring of additional paraphernalia. It was voted that the transfer be made on December 14th, or as soon thereafter as possible. At this meeting the door of Scottish Rite Masonry was opened to several Brothers whose assistance was to prove valuable in furthering the interests of the Lodge. In fact the little class of eight who received the degree of Secret Master, that evening, was in some respects the most important ever introduced into Palmoni Lodge room. It consisted of Walter D. Greene, William J. Gunnell, Francis G. Ward, Arthur L. Knight, George D. Hayes, Louis P. Adolff, Jr., Charles E. Hayes and Henry M. Barker. They were instructed in the secrets of the 14th degree on February 25, 1892.

In its new quarters, Palmoni Lodge took on renewed activity. At the election of 1892 the official line was retained, more paraphernalia was procured and the work of exemplification was extended. At the meeting on Thursday, February 25th, twenty-eight candidates were passed to full membership, taking the vow of fealty. At the meeting held on March 29th, revised and comprehensive by-laws were adopted, the same having been made to conform with the requirements of the Supreme Council. Thus, in every possible way, were the energetic officers preparing the organization for the great work before it, scarcely dreaming of the enormous proportions it was later to assume.

A Memorable Year.

The election of 1893, the year which was to prove memorable owing to the organization of the Consistory, was held on Tuesday evening, January 25th. Ill. Brother Cushman, having in mind the work of organization declined to accept a re-election to the office of Thrice Potent Master, and George L. Brown was advanced to that position. Charles E. Markham was elected Senior Warden and Walter D. Greene, Junior Warden. The new officers were installed by Ill. Charles W. Cushman. As a mark of appreciation of the untiring activity of the retiring Master and the success which had attended his efforts on behalf of the Lodge, Brother A. Oppenheimer moved that Ill. Brother Cushman be presented with a 32d degree ring, and a committee composed of A. Oppenheimer, Horace A. Noble, and George L. Kingston was appointed to procure the same.

When the report of the secretary was read at the stated communication on February 28, 1893, it showed the Lodge to be in greatly improved condition, both financially, and in the matter of increased membership. It gave every evidence of continued prosperity. This improvement called for a more thorough business organization. There was more complication of the affairs of the organization with the addition of the two higher bodies, the Rose Croix and Consistory. A new section was added to the by-laws, providing that the Thrice Potent Master of Palmoni Lodge, the Sovereign Prince of Palmoni Council, the Most Wise Master of Buffalo Chapter of the Rose Croix and the Commander-in-Chief of Buffalo Consistory, constitute a board of trustees, whose duty should be "to examine the books, vouchers, etc., of the treasurer and secretary from time to time; also to examine all bills, accounts and claims that may be presented to the Lodge for payment. They shall have charge of the funds and properties of the Lodge, and shall make such use of the same, with the sanction of the bodies, as may be deemed advisable. They may make such purchases of paraphernalia and properties, for the better working of the several grades, as the necessities of the case may require and the condition of the funds will warrant."

Owing to the increased clerical work of the Lodge, the Thrice Potent Master was authorized and directed to appoint an Assistant Secretary. A surprise, agreeable as unexpected, came to the members when Horace A. Noble, on behalf of the Lodge, presented to Ill. Charles W. Cushman, in lieu of the ring which had been proposed, a beautiful silver tea service, in appreciation of his labors in the lodge during the preceding two years. Louis P. Adolff, Jr., was then installed as Grand Master of Ceremonies.

Much Credit Due.

Following the first annual reunion, which opened on Monday, May 29, 1903, and was held mainly to celebrate the establishment of the Chapter and Consistory, the work of the four bodies has been so interwoven, as to require no separate record here, beyond the special incidents affecting the particular body under consideration. The more important events in the history of the Scottish Rite following the reorganization and consolidation of 1893, have already been chronicled in the record of the higher body. But in a study of the development and progress of the Orient of Buffalo, it should be borne in mind that to the Lodge of Perfection must be given a large portion of the credit, for what has been and will hereafter, be accomplished. It is the narrow door, through which all must pass, and upon its officers depends largely the character of the material, wrought into the complete Masonic edifice.

At the annual election held on January 5, 1894, all the officers retained their positions. The work of the year had been most satisfactory. A Finance Committee, composed of Frank S. Coit, Tellico Johnson and N. O. Tiffany, was appointed. Installation of officers was conducted by Ill. Charles W. Cushman, assisted by the other officers of Buffalo Consistory.

In his annual address delivered in presence of the four Bodies, Ill. Brother Cushman detailed the steps which had been taken to secure the enlarged organization, and praised unstintedly the officers of the several Bodies, who had so loyally cooperated with him in the work of extension. He cautioned the greatest care in the selection of members, of the four Bodies, to the end that they might be raised to the highest standard in the craft. An address was also delivered by Ill. John

Hodge, 33° Active, Deputy for New York, which reflected the greatest good will. Among other things, he said:

"It is the true nobility of Freemasonry that has established it upon the Rock of Ages, and that gives to it a lasting place in the world's history. The inherent purity of the lessons of the lodge-room shine brightly above all other things, and that is the foundation upon which its past glorious history rests, and that, too, is the hope we have for its existence in the future."

WORK IS COMMENDED.

The annual meeting of Palmoni Lodge for 1895 was held in Masonic Temple, on February 1st. At this meeting Ill. Brother Cushman introduced the following resolution, relative to the acceptance by the Supreme Council of Grand Inspectors General, of the invitation, to hold its eighty-third annual session in the Valley of Buffalo, on the third Tuesday of September, 1895:

"Resolved that it is the sense of this meeting that the four heads of the Scottish Rite Bodies constitute themselves an executive committee, elect officers, appoint sub-committees, and be authorized with power to expend such money for entertainment, as in their judgment may be deemed expedient." The resolution was unanimously adopted.

At the election which followed, the entire line of officers were selected to serve for the third term.

At the time of the third annual reunion in March, 1895, Palmoni Lodge was favored by the presence at its session of Ill. Brother James I. Buchanan, 33°, Active, Commander-in-Chief of Pennsylvania Consistory, and Ill. Clinton F. Paige, 33°, Active, Grand Secretary General of the Supreme Council. Both spoke at some length upon the important lessons taught in the Lodge of Perfection degrees, and highly commended the officers of Palmoni Lodge on the efficiency and impressiveness of their work. Horace A. Noble thanked the distinguished visitors for their presence and their kind words.

Report of the secretary made on May 3, 1895, showed a membership in the Lodge of 363, Palmoni Council 338, Buffalo Chapter of Rose Croix 274 and Buffalo Consistory, 269.

A constitutional communication of Palmoni Lodge of Perfection was held on Monday evening, June 24, 1895, together with the co-ordinate bodies of the Rite, in commemoration of the Nativity of St. John the Baptist, Brother George L. Brown, Thrice Potent Master, presiding. There was a large attendance of members and their ladies. Prayer was offered by the Grand Orator, Brother John L. Brothers and the choir rendered a suitable selection. The Thrice Potent Master declared the Lodge informally opened and introduced the Rev. Charles C. Albertson, who delivered a masterly address, entirely in keeping with the occasion. Exercises closed with singing by the choir and the benediction. An informal reception followed. Thus established, celebration of the feast day has been continued, as a regular annual feature of Palmoni Lodge.

HISTORY OF BUFFALO CONSISTORY

At a stated communication held on September 6, 1895, the question of the assessment levied by Rochester Consistory, upon the members withdrawing from that body to unite with Buffalo Consistory, was taken up, the report of the joint committee being received and acted upon. Rochester's loss by the organization of the Buffalo body, amounted to 126 members. In accordance with the report of the joint committee, it was voted to pay Rochester Consistory $4, for each member thus transferred. The members subject to this assessment and who constituted the Buffalo Consistory charter list, were: William L. Alexander, Henry Altman, Charles H. Armstrong, Louis P. Adolff, Jr., Thomas C. Burns, Fred Busch, J. Peter Braner, George J. Bailey, John L. Brothers, James W. Burke, R. H. Bickford, Charles F. Bishop, George L. Brown, Harlow W. Bailey, William M. Bloomer, George F. Brownell, Mark W. Cole, George W. Crosier, Adam Cornelius, George H. Clarke, William Cronyn, Frank S. Coit, Charles W. Cushman, Henry R. Clark, James Chalmers, Horace D. Cary, Sherman L. Cary, William C. Colwell, Charles H. Corbett, Charles J. Close, Edward E. Coatsworth, William Christian, Brad J. Cilley, Francis T. Coppins, Charles R. Dunning, William H. Dick, Robert Denton, Charles A. DeLaney, David F. Day, George A. Davis, Wells Dygert, Charles W. Fuller, Charles H. Fennell, Fred W. Fisher, Henry G. Falke, James A. Given, Stephen S. Greene, Charles F. Gehring, George J. H. Goehler, Ole E. Goldhagen, Walter D. Greene,

LADIES' ROOM, FURNISHED BY CLASS OF 1915

ANCIENT ACCEPTED SCOTTISH RITE

Philip Hoenig, Charles P. Hohlstein, William Hengerer, Charles Heinold, Wilbur N. Hoag, Frank Hammond, James M. Henderson, Henry Haier, Frank P. Haggerty, Charles E. Hayes, George D. Hayes, James C. Holiday, Timothy W. Jackson, Avery D. Jones, Edgar B. Jewett, Tellico Johnson, Louis H. Knapp, William H. Kurtz, Eugene S. Knapp, George L. Kingston, Henry G. Knapp, Arthur L. Knight, Henry H. Little, Daniel N. Lockwood, Daniel H. McWilliams, Emil Mackwirth, Darius E. Morgan, James J. MacKenzie, Albert E. Miller, John Malcolm, Charles E. Markham, John Masters, Jr., Horace A. Noble, Orin G. Nichols, Abram Oppenheimer, Wallace Prouty, Abraham B. Perren, Joel H. Prescott, James H. Preston, James W. Ruger, Perry C. Reyburn, Samuel Root, William J. Runcie, John Reining, Jr., G. Barrett Rich, Clark H. Rice, William H. Rice, N. Worth Ransom, George Reimann, Henry Smith, Andrew Shiels, Henry Smith 2d, Jacob Stern, Frank E. Shaw, Elroy F. Sabin, Henry Schafer, John Slote, Matthew Thielen, James H. Tifft, Robert C. Titus, Grant H. Thompson, Millard F. Tallmadge, Theodore L. Wadsworth, Charles G. Worthington, James L. Walker, Fred Wagner, Robert T. Walker, Ira C. Woodward, Francis G. Ward, Charles H. Webster, Matthew G. Weber, George H. Young, Robert D. Young, William J. Ziegele.

SUPREME COUNCIL MEETING.

An occasion of importance to all the Scottish Rite bodies of Buffalo, was the meeting of the

Supreme Council which convened for three days in the Valley of Buffalo, September 17th, 18th and 19th, 1895. Not only was the event marked by a round of pleasant excursions, in the hours not devoted to the work of the Council, and which the committee had provided in attractive form, but four brothers of Buffalo Consistory were honored by being received, welcomed and proclaimed Sovereign Grand Inspectors General, and enrolled as honorary members of the Supreme Council. They were Ill. Horace A. Noble, Ill. Robert C. Titus, Ill. John L. Brothers and Ill. George L. Brown. Prince Edward W. Hatch was elected to receive the high honor at the next annual session. It was an occasion long to be remembered by the participants and of great benefit to the Rite in the Valley of Buffalo, as serving to bring the Buffalo bodies into closer, more intimate relation with the Grand Body, and demonstrate to the latter the substantial character of the organization effected by the Buffalo adherents of the Scottish Rite.

The twenty-ninth annual meeting of Palmoni Lodge was held February 7, 1896. Walter D. Greene was elected Thrice Potent Master, L. P. Adolff, Jr., Deputy Master; Joseph Fowler, Senior Warden; T. Haven Ross, Junior Warden; John L. Brothers, Orator; Samuel Root, Treasurer and Charles E. Markham, Secretary. They were installed by Ill. George L. Brown at the succeeding communication, Brother Joel H. Prescott officiating as Grand Marshal. Secretary's report showed a total membership of 404; Palmoni Council, 369, Buffalo Rose Croix, 346 and Buffalo Consistory, 341. At the election held on February 5, 1897, no change was made in the personnel of the officers named above.

Only one change was made in the elective officers at the beginning of 1888. Morris Benson being substituted for T. Haven Ross as Junior Grand Warden. At the annual election of 1899, Louis P. Adolff, Jr., was advanced to the office of Thrice Potent Master and his associate officers promoted in like degree. Lawrence T. Hammond was elected Junior Grand Warden and Charles W. Mann was appointed Grand Master of Ceremonies. Brother Walter D. Greene officiated as installing officer. The election of 1900 made no change in this list.

Date Of A Tragedy.

On February 1, 1901, the officers were advanced one station each, Brother Joseph Fowler becoming Thrice Potent Master. Brother Charles W. Mann was elected Junior Grand Warden. Almon H. Roudebush was appointed Master of Ceremonies and Martin H. Blecher, Captain of the Guard. The officers were installed by Ill. Charles W. Cushman.

At the regular communication of Palmoni Lodge held on September 6, 1901, the date of a National tragedy, the following resolution was offered by Ill. Commander-in-Chief Cushman and unanimously adopted:

"Resolved That it is the sense of all of us assembled here, that we deeply deplore what has occurred this afternoon and that we tender the heartfelt sympathy of the Scottish Rite Masons of Buffalo, to the beloved wife and family of our dear President, William McKinley."

Owing to the remarkable growth of the Scottish Rite bodies, the limited quarters in the Masonic Temple, had, by this time, become entirely inadequate for a satisfactory presentation of the work, and the consent of the Lodge was accorded unanimously to Ill. Brother Cushman, at his request, to employ an architect to draw plans for new quarters, the plans to be retained for subsequent use, after being submitted for the approval of the trustees.

Approval of the officers and their work during 1901 was expressed by their retention in their respective stations for 1902. At a meeting on April 4, 1902, a committee of three was appointed to take under consideration the subject of providing more commodious quarters for the several bodies of the Rite. Such committee was composed of Ill. Charles W. Cushman, chairman, Joel H. Prescott, Jr., Joseph Fowler and George H. Woolley.

At the election in 1903, held February 6, Charles W. Mann was elected Senior Grand Warden and George K. Staples was advanced to the position of Orator, Ill. John L. Brothers retiring from the line. No other changes were made in the elective list. Martin H. Blecher was appointed Master of Ceremonies.

ANCIENT ACCEPTED SCOTTISH RITE

An interesting occasion was the regular communication held on April 3, 1903. At that time Brother Abram Oppenheimer, whose early efforts for the maintenance of Palmoni Lodge had given him a prominent place in the records of the organization, was present, and entertained the members with a most interesting address, relative to the early history of the Lodge, previous to the Miller-Greiner building fire. Brother Oppenheimer, was largely responsible for the reorganization of the Lodge after the fire, which destroyed all the books, records and paraphernalia of the lodge, practically wiping it out as an organization, being the first Master elected after the disaster. He enjoyed the unusual privilege of selecting the balance of the officers after he had himself been elected Thrice Potent Master. His story of the struggles, trials and disappointments of the early days was a revelation to the members, who had known only the more prosperous period. From the ruins of the Miller-Greiner fire Brother Oppenheimer had recovered the fraternal box, containing the coins which had been collected for charity, on the last meeting night previous to the fire. These coins he had carefully preserved and they were now presented as souvenirs to those brothers who had been members of Palmoni Lodge at the time of the fire. They were thirty-nine in number.

At the election held on February 5, 1904, Morris Benson was chosen Thrice Potent Master; Charles W. Mann, Deputy Master; Martin H. Blecher, Senior Grand Warden; Otto W. Volger, Junior

Grand Warden; George K. Staples, Orator. Samuel Root and Charles E. Markham were retained as Treasurer and Secretary respectively. Brother Benson retained the office of Thrice Potent Master only one year, retiring at the election in 1905, the remaining officers each being advanced one station. William H. Bradish was elected Orator and Thrice Potent Master Mann appointed Brother Charles H. Andrews, Master of Ceremonies. Installation was conducted by Ill. George L. Brown. Similar action was taken at the annual meeting in February, 1906, Martin H. Blecher taking the chair of Thrice Potent. Walter F. Gibson was appointed Master of Ceremonies and George A. Halbin, Captain of the Guard.

First Cathedral Meeting.

Palmoni Lodge came into its own on Monday, April 23, 1906, at which time the first session of the Lodge in the Delaware Avenue Cathedral was held. As the older members assembled in the spacious lodge-room and contemplated the extensive alterations which had been effected, to afford them a suitable home, their minds must have traveled back to those other days, so fraught with hardships and dread of the future, which at that time gave so little promise of success. And reflecting on those darker days, there must have come a sublime satisfaction that they had proven loyal and had stood manfully at their posts when the storms of censure, strife and adversity, had sought to overwhelm their nearly stranded Masonic bark. Here, at last, they were landed in a safe, commodious and beautiful harbor, where the tempest of opposition and the storms of rivalry, could make no impression. The fondest ambition of Abram Oppenheimer, of Brothers and Root, of Cushman and Brown, were surely realized in this beautiful lodge room, fitted in every way to carry on the impressive work of the order in its superlative beauty.

Presentation Of A Bible.

In presenting a Bible to the Consistory and co-ordinate bodies, on this occasion, Martin H. Blecher, Thrice Potent Master of Palmoni Lodge, said:

"Ill. Commander-in-Chief:—

"This vast assemblage of Brother Scottish Rite Masons, is an evidence and an expression of their loyalty and devotion for our beloved Rite. It is an indication that they feel very proud of this magnificent edifice which will henceforth be their home, pronounced the finest Cathedral of its kind in the United States, and soon to be consecrated and dedicated to the service of the Great Jehovah and Scottish Rite Masonry forever. Illustrious Commander-in-Chief, through the untiring efforts of our building committee, consisting of yourself and your associates the Illustrious Brother Prescott and the Illustrious Brother Titus, their zeal and devotion to the Rite, they have made great personal sacrifices and made it possible for us to assemble here tonight, in this our new home. Illustrious Commander-in-Chief, on behalf of the brethren of Palmoni Lodge of Perfection, I congratulate your committee on their well-deserved success, and convey to you the sincere and heartfelt thanks and the assurance of their highest appreciation of your noble efforts. In their behalf your names will be perpetuated by Buffalo Consistory. Your committee may well be proud of their achievement, for the brethren are very proud indeed of their committee. Illustrious Commander-in-Chief, a word for myself. This is the proudest moment of my life, for I consider it a most distinguished honor to have the privilege of presiding at the opening of this the first reunion held in this beautiful Cathedral. It is also the turning of the tenth milestone of my membership in Buffalo consistory. During this period of years the brethren have been very kind to me. At all times have they extended to me that hearty Masonic welcome for which the brethren of Buffalo Consistory are well known. The brethren conferred a distinguished honor upon me by electing me their Thrice Potent Grand Master, an honor which I prize very highly, because the high office came to me unsolicited, as have all my Masonic honors come to me in the past. For all of which I feel deeply indebted to the brothers of Buffalo Consistory and beg to extend to them hearty and sincere thanks, and as a token of esteem and appreciation, I ask you, Illustrious Commander-in-Chief, to accept from my hands the Holy Bible, Square and Compasses, and I pray that our Heavenly Father may grant to you, Illustrious Sir, and to every member of Buffalo Consistory, his choicest blessings, peace and happiness for many years to come, to enable us to drink the living waters from this ever-flowing fountain of truth, and when the summons shall finally come, and the Great Architect of the Universe shall call us home, may we be found worthy to enjoy life everlasting in the glorious Consistory above.''

Ill. Francis G. Ward, on behalf of the Consistory, expressed his acceptance and appreciation, by promptly displaying the great lights.

On the occasion of the celebration of St. John the Evangelist's Day, on Thursday evening, December 27, 1906, a delegation from Niagara Lodge of Perfection, headed by Ill. Brother A. H. G. Hardwicke, was present, as also were a large delegation of Past Thrice Potent Masters of Palmoni Lodge. They were greeted by Thrice Potent Master Blecher, who gave a brief history of Palmoni Lodge and welcomed them to the East. Members of the Supreme Council were also received and welcomed and Ill. Robert C. Titus delivered a short address on Scottish Rite Masonry. The Rev. Darius H. Muller spoke on the subject of St. John the Evangelist. The 14th degree Grand Elect Mason was conferred upon a class of sixteen, in full form and ceremony.

FORTIETH ANNIVERSARY.

The Fortieth Anniversary of the institution of Palmoni Lodge of Perfection and Palmoni Council Princes of Jerusalem, was observed at a special communication held on May 24, 1907. At this session also, the officers elected on May 3d, were installed by Ill. Francis G. Ward, assisted by Ill. William H. Lyons, as Grand Marshal. No changes had been made in the personnel of the officers. Following the installation the following program was carried out, in honor of the Lodge and Council, which by their unselfish and determined efforts during the forty years of their existence, had made the organization and success of the Consistory possible. Invocation by the Rev. Henry Ward; Address by Thrice Potent Master Blecher; Reminiscent talks by Past Thrice Potent Masters, Abram Oppenheimer, Mark W. Cole, Joseph Fowler, and Charles W. Mann. Musical selections by the chorister. Remarks by Walter M. Zink, Sovereign Prince of Palmoni Council and Rev. Darius H. Muller. A telegram signed by Ill. John Lloyd Thomas, Commander-in-Chief of New York City Consistory, congratulating Lodge and Council on their fortieth anniversary, was read.

At the election held on May 1, 1908, Otto W. Volger was advanced to the position of Thrice Potent Master. The other officers were retained being regularly advanced. Brother Charles I. Heckman, present Thrice Potent Master, and one of the most earnest workers the Lodge has ever honored, was appointed Master of Ceremonies. The same officers were returned to their several stations at the election on May 7, 1909.

On May 6, 1910, Brother George K. Staples, present Commander-in-Chief, was unanimously elected Thrice Potent Master and his associate officers advanced at each station. Levi R. Cooper was appointed Master of Ceremonies, thus taking his place in the regular line of progression. E. Bert Henshaw was appointed Guard. Officers were installed by Ill. Francis G. Ward, assisted by Brother Charles W. Mann, as Marshal.

ANCIENT ACCEPTED SCOTTISH RITE

The first constitutional Lodge of Sorrow, was held in Palmoni Lodge, on Friday evening, November 4, 1910, Thrice Potent George K. Staples presiding, with Martin H. Blecher, as King Solomon; Charles H. Andrews, Grand Inspector; Walter F. Gibson, Senior Warden; Henry C. Cassler, Orator; Levi R. Cooper, Master of Ceremonies; George H. Clarke, Tiler; Charles I. Heckman, Captain of the Guard, with the following guards: Robert Bruce, Carl H. Debus, William J. Flierl, Wilbur H. Funk, George A. Oehler, Howard F. Smith, John Moore, Charles F. Zimmerman, Jacob Harris, Adam H. Debus, George H. Cotter and John G. Marks. The exercises were impressive. An organ solo was followed by opening of the lodge by the Master and his associate officers, an invocation by the Rev. Henry C. Cassler, a hymn, "Nearer My God to Thee" by the entire assembly, and an address by Brother Charles Elbert Rhodes. Memorial services were conducted by the following: First arch, James L. Nixon; second arch, E. Bert Henshaw; third arch, George L. Brown; fourth arch, Levi R. Cooper; fifth arch, Charles W. Mann. Processionals and musical selections constituted the second section of the services, closing with the benediction.

HONOR PAST OFFICERS.

Palmoni Lodge has enjoyed many pleasant social affairs, but probably none more thoroughly than the reception to its Past Thrice Potent

Masters, held on March 31, 1911. This was another of the innovations introduced by Thrice Potent George K. Staples, whose desire to stimulate interest among the members has found expression in a multitude of ways. Up to this time Palmoni Lodge had honored fifteen presiding officers. George C. Pennell, the first Thrice Potent had withdrawn; four, James McCredie, George M. Osgoodby, Charles W. Cushman and Joseph Fowler had been summoned by the Grand Master Architect. Following the reception of the surviving Past Thrice Potents by the Master, who spoke of the great work which they had accomplished in glowing terms of praise, and a brief history of Palmoni Lodge by Secretary Harry D. Hosmer, adjournment was taken to the banquet hall. Thrice Potent Master Staples presided as toast master, and good cheer and good fellowship ruled until a late hour.

At the annual election in 1911, the officers were returned for a second term, holding their relative positions, and Harry D. Hosmer who had been Acting Secretary during the illness of Ill. Brother Markham, was elected Secretary. The work of the year had been the most satisfactory in the history of the Lodge. The success attained by the Lodge during the first year of Brother Staples' administration was even more pronounced during his succeeding term, and when he surrendered the office of Thrice Potent Master to Brother Charles H. Andrews, on May 3, 1912, he left a record of which any presiding officer might well be proud. With Brother Andrews and his former associate officers, was installed Thomas H. Noonan as Orator and George Clinton, Jr., Master of Ceremonies.

BUYING A HOME SITE.

On June 7, 1912, favorable action was taken upon the proposition to purchase the Blocher property, and the Trustees were instructed to take necessary steps to transfer the property to Buffalo Consistory. The vote was unanimous. The Secretary's report showed that the membership of Palmoni Lodge on June 7, 1912, was 1403, a net gain for the year of 196; Palmoni Council 1501, a net gain of 205; Buffalo Chapter Rose Croix, 1692, a net gain of 219 and Buffalo Consistory, 1693, a net gain of 220. That the increase in the Consistory was greater than in the Lodge, was due to the fact that the jurisdiction of the Consistory extended beyond that of the Lodge, embracing territory in the counties of Genesee, Wyoming, Allegheny, Chautauqua, Cattaraugus, Livingston, Niagara, Erie and Orleans.

At the meeting on September 6th, announcement was made of the death of Ill. Christopher G. Fox, with the exception of Brother William Mullen, the last survivor of the original charter members of Palmoni Lodge.

At his own request Thrice Potent Master Charles H. Andrews was not considered as a candidate to succeed himself, and at the annual election in 1913, Brother Walter F. Gibson was advanced to the responsible station. Thomas H. Noonan was elected Junior Warden and Louis H. Rathman, Orator. Brother Burton E. Pfeiffer was appointed Master of Ceremonies. The election was held on May 21st. Both Brother Noonan and Brother Rathman resigned and at a special election to fill vacancies, held on June 6th, both were re-elected, Brother Rathman as Junior Warden and Brother Noonan as Orator, each accepting the changed position. The officers were installed by Ill. Charles W. Mann, assisted by Brother Charles H. Andrews. The year had been prosperous, showing a gain of 290 initiates, with a net gain in membership of 233. At the election of 1914, the confidence of the members in these officers was emphasized by their return to their several stations.

PRESENTED LIFE MEMBERSHIP.

At the regular communication held on June 5, 1914, there was present, Ill. George Moore, 33°, Commander-in-Chief of Moore Consistory, Hamilton, Ont., Ill. Frederick R. Smith, 33°, Past Commander of Rochester Consistory and Ill. Frederick S. Parkhurst, 33°. They were elected to honorary membership in the Buffalo Bodies. Again at the meeting of September 4, 1914, the Lodge was honored by the presence of two distinguished guests—Ill. Benjamin Allen, 33°, Sovereign Grand Commander of the Supreme Council of Canada, and Ill. Lewis F. Riggs, 33°, Grand Secretary of the same body. On September 11th, on motion of Ill. George K. Staples, Ill. Samuel Root was made a life member of all the Scottish Rite bodies of Buffalo. It was a well-deserved compliment to the faithful performance of duty and of the veteran treasurer's fidelity and long service. The hope was universal and hearty that this, oldest officer of the Rite in the Valley of Buffalo, may for years enjoy the health necessary to permit him to continue the duties he has so well performed for twenty-six years. On November 6th, Brother Gerald D. Bliss presented to the Lodge a book giving the Masonic history of the brothers located in the Canal Zone, Isthmus of Panama. It was accepted by Commander-in-Chief Staples, with appropriate expressions of pleasure and thanks.

On January 8, 1915, at the regular communication of the Lodge, on motion of Ill. George K. Staples, Commander-in-Chief of the Consistory, Ill. Brother Andrew Shiels, 33°, and Ill. Brother George H. Clarke, 33°, were honored by being made life members of Buffalo Consistory. Both of these loyal brothers were among the earliest initiates of Palmoni Lodge, joining previous to 1882, and serving in their respective positions of Hospitaler and Sentinel, for many years.

Present Directing Forces.

At the annual election of officers held on May 1, 1915, the several officers were advanced by unanimous vote of the Lodge, Brother Walter F. Gibson retiring from the office of Thrice Potent

Master. The following were chosen and at this writing, December 31, 1915, are the active directing forces of the destiny of Palmoni Lodge:

Charles I. Heckman	*Thrice Potent Master*
Levi R. Cooper	*Deputy Master*
Louis H. Rathman	*Senior Warden*
John S. Embleton	*Junior Warden*
Thomas H. Noonan	*Orator*
Samuel Root	*Treasurer*
Harry D. Hosmer	*Secretary*
Burton E. Pfeiffer	*Master of Ceremonies*
Andrew Shiels	*Hospitaler*
Charles P. Smith	*Guard*
George H. Clarke	*Tiler*

A committee on revision of by-laws was appointed consisting of Ill. George K. Staples, Charles Elbert Rhodes, James L. Nixon and Charles I. Heckman. On June 4th, Ill. Francis G. Ward was made a life member of all the Buffalo Scottish Rite bodies. On July 2d the revised by-laws were approved and adopted. At this meeting there was received from Brother W. B. King, master of United Crafts Lodge, F. & A. M., a letter of thanks to the Buffalo Consistory, for the use of the Cathedral for the consecration, dedication and constitution of the new lodge. The incident served still further to demonstrate the practical obliteration of all lines of cleavage between the Symbolic and Ineffable grades of the Fraternity; to prove that the brethren of the Blue and the brothers of the Scarlet, are traveling onward together under the more intimate Purple banner of Union. The total membership of Palmoni Lodge at the close of 1915, was 2356. Fourteen brothers had crossed the dark river during the year ending June 1, 1915, and ten had demitted, making the total gain for the Masonic year, 231.

PALMONI COUNCIL

In Which the Fifteenth and Sixteenth Degrees are Conferred.
Its Organization Coincident With Palmoni Lodge.

WHILE Palmoni Council, Princes of Jerusalem, is of equal age with Palmoni Lodge of Perfection, the early history of the former rests in even greater obscurity than that of the latter. As the first available minutes of the Council are those of December 24, 1887, we are forced to depend entirely upon the memory of the oldest members, for a record of those earlier years. From that source we learn that for the first sixteen years of its existence, the Council was presided over by six different Sovereign Princes. They were George C. Pennell, who was the official head of both Lodge and Council at their inception; Lorenzo M. Kenyon, John C. Graves, Oren G. Nichols, James McCredie and Henry Waters. It has been impossible to learn in which years these respective officers served, but as the work of Lodge and Council was closely allied, it is safe to presume that the terms of service were about equally divided.

Lorenzo M. Kenyon, who was the second Sovereign Prince of Palmoni Council, like most of his associate officers, had been Master of a Blue Lodge, having served as the presiding head of the

ANCIENT ACCEPTED SCOTTISH RITE

Lodge of the Ancient Landmarks, during 1858, the year of that Lodge's institution. Brother John C. Graves had served as Master of Washington Lodge in 1878-9; Henry Waters in Hiram Lodge, in 1866; James McCredie in Erie Lodge in 1859 and Oren G. Nichols in Queen City Lodge, in 1887. Brother James McCredie appears to have been unusually active in the work of the Lodge and Council, presiding and working in both bodies.

WORKING IN HARMONY.

Brother John C. Graves, who at the time was Deputy Master of Palmoni Lodge, was elected Sovereign Prince of Palmoni Council in 1881, when George M. Osgoodby was made Thrice Potent Master of the former Body. Brother Graves was Sovereign Prince at the time of the Miller-Greiner fire, when all the records were destroyed. He has since withdrawn from the Scottish Rite bodies. At the election immediately following the fire, when Abram Oppenheimer was elected Master of Palmoni Lodge, Mark W. Cole, Deputy Master, was elected Sovereign Prince of the Council. The other stations were filled by officers of the Lodge, even the Thrice Potent Master taking any station which chanced to be vacant.

Thus the history of Palmoni Lodge, up to 1887, appears to have been the history of Palmoni Council. Certain it is that the meetings were held in the same room, on the same evenings, the work being performed practically by the same officers, the Deputy Master of the Lodge serving as Sovereign Prince of the Council. Brother Oppenheimer tells us that he received all the degrees, from the 4th to the 16th inclusive, on the same evening. What a contrast to the elaborate, detailed and impressive presentation of the work at the present time!

No explanation has been found for the fact, that while the minutes of the Lodge of Perfection have been preserved since the fire of 1882, the records of Palmoni Council previous to the close of 1887, are missing. The presumption is that they were either lost in the last fire, or had not been deemed of sufficient importance to warrant preservation. Strangely enough, the minutes of Palmoni Lodge make practically no reference to its associate Body, beyond the fact that its degrees were conferred.

First Recorded Election.

At the first recorded election of Palmoni Council, held on December 24, 1887, twenty years after the organization, the following officers were elected:

Oren G. Nichols	*Sovereign Prince*
George L. Kingston	*High Priest*
Henry Smith, 2d	*Senior Grand Warden*
Matthew Thielen	*Junior Grand Warden*
James McCredie	*Grand Treasurer*
Theodore L. Wadsworth	*Grand Secretary*

Appointments of the Sovereign Prince were:

Eugene S. Knapp	*Master of Ceremonies*
Henry A. Clark	*Captain of the Guard*
Horace A. Noble	*Hospitaler*
Charles A. Dunning	*Tiler*

ANCIENT ACCEPTED SCOTTISH RITE

Petitions were received from seven candidates, among the number being G. Barrett Rich, father of the present District Deputy of the 38th Masonic District.

At the succeeding election in 1888, Brother Nichols was returned to the Master's chair, but Horace Noble was substituted for George L. Kingston as High Priest and William H. Baker, elected Grand Treasurer. Samuel Root was started in the line by being appointed Grand Master of Entrances. These constituted the changes made at this election. On April 2, 1889, a special convocation was held for the purpose of conferring degrees. At this time the 15th degree was communicated and the 16th conferred in full form, on a class of twenty-seven candidates. Visitors were present from Albany, Jersey City and Corning.

Thus early were pleasing fraternal relations established, between the Brethren of Buffalo and those of the other cities of the state; relations which have maintained through all the years of the past and seem destined to continue through all the years to come. In Corning, especially, Buffalo Consistory and its co-ordinate bodies, stand in high esteem. This meeting was held in Parish lodge room and a vote of thanks was extended for the use of the same.

Samuel Root Appointed.

On May 25, 1889, at a stated convocation of Palmoni Council, held in the Austin building, announcement was made by the Sovereign Prince of the death of Valient Prince, William H. Baker, Grand Treasurer. Appropriate resolutions were adopted and the Sovereign Prince appointed Valient Prince Samuel Root to the office of Treasurer, to hold the same until an election could be had, the Secretary being instructed to call such an election on June 22d. It was voted to concur with the action of Palmoni Lodge of Perfection, in subscribing to and paying for, $1,000 of the income bonds of the Masonic Hall Association. An order for that sum was directed to be drawn upon the Treasurer. At the election of June 22d, the appointment of Samuel Root, as Treasurer, was ratified by his unanimous election to the office, which he has held uninterruptedly to the present.

Visit to Rochester.

On April 29, 1889, Palmoni Council officers visited Rochester and conferred the 15th and 16th degrees; Knight of the East or Sword, being communicated, and Prince of Jerusalem conferred in full form and ceremony. At the election of December, 1889, George L. Kingston was returned to his former office of High Priest, but the other officers remained unchanged. Again in 1890, there was no change, except that Charles A. DeLaney was elected Grand Senior Warden, in place of Henry Smith 2d. Few meetings of the Council were held, the principal business of the two bodies being transacted in Palmoni Lodge, and the Council convening only when there was work.

ANCIENT ACCEPTED SCOTTISH RITE

At the election held on December 26, 1891, material changes were made in the personnel of the officers. Charles A. DeLaney was elected Sovereign Prince, George L. Kingston, High Priest; George L. Brown, Senior Warden; Clark W. Rice, Junior Warden. Secretary Wadsworth and Treasurer Root were, of course, retained. The Sovereign Prince announced the appointment of the following subordinate officers: Frank Hammond, Master of Ceremonies; Charles E. Markham, Master of Entrances; Andrew Shiels, Almoner, and William Christian, Tiler. No change in these officers was made in 1892, except that Charles E. Hayes was substituted for Frank Hammond, as Master of Ceremonies. At the meeting of April 28, 1892, resolutions of sympathy were drafted, extending the deep regret of the Buffalo brethren, at the loss by fire, of the Rochester Masonic Temple.

Meetings Well Attended.

At the annual meeting held on December 22, 1892, announcement was made of the death of Prince Hawley Kline, and Brother John C. Graves and Secretary T. L. Wadsworth were appointed a committee to draft suitable memorial. It is noticeable that the Council meetings were well attended, many of the earlier members of the bodies maintaining their loyalty, and lending encouragement to the officers by their presence, ready to assist in any way to further the interests of the Council. Among the familiar names found upon the minute book of this period are those of Charles W. Cushman, Henry Smith 2d, Ole E. Goldhagen, Louis P. Adolff, Jr., Henry Schafer, William J. Cronyn, Henry Haier, George H. Clarke, Horace A. Noble, Tellico Johnson, Abram Oppenheimer and many others.

At the election held on December 8, 1893, all of the elective officers were retained, with the exception of George L. Brown, who declined re-election. Louis P. Adolff, Jr., was chosen Junior Grand Warden, that station being vacant by the advancement of Clark W. Rice to the office of Senior Warden, George L. Kingston becoming High Priest. In the appointive list, John Malcolm was made Master of Wardrobe, George J. Metzger, Engineer and Architect, Robert Denton, Organist and Alvin W. Day Master of Entrances. John Malcolm was also appointed Tiler.

IN THE MONTH TEBETH.

In the following year, the date of election was changed from December to January, the selection of officers for 1895 being made on January 11th of that year. Reason for this is found in the regulations which provided that elections of officers of Councils, Princes of Jerusalem, must be held at the stated meeting on, or next preceding, the 20th day of the Hebrew month Tebeth. All the officers of 1894 were returned to their respective stations. The same officers were again returned in 1896, but owing to absence from the city, Brother Theodore L. Wadsworth declined the office of Secretary, and

ILL. GEORGE H. CLARKE, 33°
LIFE MEMBER OF BUFFALO CONSISTORY; A CHARTER MEMBER AND ITS
GRAND SENTINEL FOR ALL THE YEARS OF ITS EXISTENCE

Charles E. Markham was appointed to fill vacancy, later being elected to the position. which he filled so capably until the time of his death.

The thirtieth annual convocation of Palmoni Council was held on December 11, 1896, the officers for 1897 being selected at this time. Prince Charles A. Delaney was, for the sixth time, selected to preside over the destinies of the Council, and all the other officers were retained in their respective stations. On December 10, 1897, these officers were chosen for 1898.

CHANGE IN OFFICERS.

At the thirty-second annual convocation of Palmoni Council, held on December 9, 1898, a complete change was made in the list of elective officers, with the exception of Secretary and Treasurer, Ill. Charles A. DeLaney retiring after a continuous service, as the Council's presiding officer, of seven years. His administration had been marked by the same efficiency and zeal for the craft which had characterized his services as Thrice Potent Master of Palmoni Lodge. The new officers elected at this convocation were Charles E. Hayes, Sovereign Prince; George H. Woolley, High Priest; Lawrence T. Hammond, Senior Warden; Charles Lee Abel, Junior Warden. The Sovereign Grand Master declared the Sovereign Prince elect duly installed into office. A special dispensation was obtained for the installation of officers on January 27, 1899, and the ceremony was conducted by Ill. Horace A. Noble, assisted by associate officers of the Lodge. Thomas Penney was installed as Master of Ceremonies and George J. Volger as Master of Entrances.

At the election held on December 8, 1899, George H. Woolley was advanced to the station of Sovereign Prince and Thomas Penney to that of High Priest. Charles Lee Abel was made Senior Warden and George J. Volger, Junior Warden. William H. Hotchkiss was appointed Master of Ceremonies and Edwin P. Sears Master of Entrances. All these officers were returned to their stations at the election of 1900, and again in 1901, with the exception of Brother Thomas Penney, who retired, his place as High Priest being taken by Brother Frank T. Gilbert. William Palmer was appointed Master of Entrances.

For the Third Term.

Again in the election for 1903, there was a change in the office of High Priest, William H. Hotchkiss being advanced and Charles S. Butler being elected Junior Warden. Charles H. Riggs was appointed Master of Ceremonies and Harry W. Crabbs, Master of Entrances. No change occurred in the official list at the election on January 8, 1904.

At the election held on December 9, 1905, the Sovereign Prince called upon Ill. Francis G. Ward to preside, who appointed Ill. Robert C. Titus and Ill. George L. Brown tellers. Brother William H. Hotchkiss was elected Sovereign Prince and the other officers were advanced, Harry W. Crabbs being elected Junior Warden. Edward K. Emory was appointed Master of Ceremonies and Thomas E. Boyd, Master of Entrances. On January 12, 1906, Brother Hotchkiss was elected for the third term as Sovereign Prince, Thomas E. Boyd was advanced to the office of Junior Warden, Brother Harry W. Crabbs having retired, and Brother Eugene Warner was appointed Master of Entrances.

DATE OF ELECTION CHANGED.

At the annual convocation of the Council held May 10, 1907, a pronounced change in the personnel of the officers was again wrought. By action of the Supreme Council, the date of election had been moved from January to May, to follow the annual Consistory reunions. At this election there were chosen the following officers, men who have brought the work of Palmoni Council up to a high state of perfection: Walter M. Zink, Sovereign Prince; Albert H. Zink, High Priest; Charles S. Butler, Senior Warden; William H. Ellis, Junior Warden. Treasurer Root and Secretary Markham were returned. Installation was deferred until May 24th, at which time the Fortieth Anniversary of Palmoni Lodge of Perfection and Palmoni Council was to be observed. At the anniversary celebration, at which the Lodge and Council attended jointly, the officers of both bodies were installed by Ill. Francis G. Ward. At this time, Brother Charles S. Butler, who had been elected Junior Warden, presented his declination of the office. At a special election to fill vacancies, held December 13th of that year, William H. Ellis was chosen Senior Warden; Charles Elbert Rhodes, Junior Warden and Byron B. Daggett was appointed Master of Ceremonies. These officers were duly installed by Sovereign Prince Walter M. Zink.

Brother Rhodes Retires.

At the election of May, 1908, the officers of the previous year were returned, with the exception of Charles Elbert Rhodes, who retired from the office of Junior Warden, his place being taken by Byron B. Daggett. William D. Camp was appointed Master of Ceremonies.

In 1909 Albert H. Zink succeeded his brother, Walter, as Sovereign Prince, and the other officers were each advanced one station. At this election William D. Camp was chosen Junior Warden and Eugene Warner was appointed Master of Ceremonies. These officers were returned in 1910, with the exception of William D. Camp, who retired to take the position of Assistant Secretary of the joint bodies. Eugene Warner was elected Junior Warden and James L. Nixon was appointed Master of Ceremonies. The officers elected and appointed were installed by Past Sovereign Prince Walter M. Zink, assisted by Brother Charles W. Mann. Following a custom, now well established, Sovereign Prince Albert H. Zink declined to consider a re-election for a third term,

ANCIENT ACCEPTED SCOTTISH RITE

and in 1911, William H. Ellis was advanced to the station of Sovereign Prince. All the other officers were advanced, James L. Nixon being elected Junior Warden. Edward D. Peters was appointed Master of Ceremonies and Wilbur H. Funk, Master of Entrances. The officers were installed by the retiring Sovereign Prince, whose services as a presiding officer had proven as valuable to the Council, as had his unselfish and always ready acceptance of any duty required of him, added to the interest and benefit of all the bodies of the Scottish Rite in Buffalo.

DEATH CAUSES CHANGES.

In the following year the above named officers were returned without change in any particular. In 1913, Byron B. Daggett was elected Sovereign Prince; James L. Nixon, High Priest; Edward D. Peters, Senior Warden; Wilbur H. Funk, Junior Warden. Albert R. Pankow was appointed Master of Ceremonies, and Philip M. Scheeler, Master of Entrances. At the succeeding election of 1914, these officers were returned, with the exception of the promotions of Brothers Wilbur H. Funk and Albert R. Pankow, owing to the death of Senior Warden Edward C. Peters. In the death of Brother Peters, the Council and the Consistory lost an active and faithful member. He had been the presiding officer in the exemplification of the 23d degree, Prince of the Tabernacle, and in honor of his memory, it was provided that the degree should not be presented for a full year.

HISTORY OF BUFFALO CONSISTORY

The year 1915 was without important event beyond the election, which took place on May 14th. Sovereign Prince, Byron B. Daggett, had been absent for several months, having business relations which called him to San Francisco during the Exposition, but no change was made in the official family until the regular annual meeting. At that time the following officers, still holding, were unanimously chosen:

James L. Nixon	*Sovereign Prince*
Wilbur H. Funk	*High Priest*
Albert R. Pankow	*Senior Warden*
Philip M. Scheeler	*Junior Warden*
Samuel Root	*Treasurer*
Harry D. Hosmer	*Secretary*
George A. Halbin	*Master of Ceremonies*
Andrew Shiels	*Hospitaler*
Charles J. Roesser	*Master of Entrances*
George H. Clarke	*Tiler*

The total membership of Palmoni Council at the close of 1915 was 2,466. The net gain to the close of the Masonic year, June 1, 1915, was 231.

BUFFALO CHAPTER

Knights of Rose Croix. Important Body in Which Seventeenth and Eighteenth Degrees are Presented.

THE organization of Buffalo Chapter of Rose Croix was coincident with that of Buffalo Consistory, charter of the two bodies being granted by the Supreme Council at the same time, in 1903. With the exception of the lists of officers who by their earnest efforts have served to encourage and stimulate interest in the beautiful work of the 17th and 18th degrees, practically all the history of the Buffalo Chapter has been already written. This does not mean that lesser importance attaches to this body than to the Council, or even the Lodge of Perfection, for the Chapter is one of the chief supports of the Scottish Rite edifice, and Buffalo Chapter has gained and maintains a high standing among the most progressive bodies of the Rite in this country. It is not too much to say that its officers, from its organization, have sought to instill into the degree work all the impressiveness, beauty and inspirational sentiment, which its ritual permits.

UNDER DISPENSATION.

The first meeting of Buffalo Chapter, under dispensation, was held in Masonic Temple on

January 6, 1893. There were present on that occasion, officers under dispensation, John L. Brothers, Most Wise Master; Charles E. Hayes, Knight Senior Warden; Joel H. Prescott, Knight Junior Warden, and the following brothers: Jacob Stern, Frank S. Coit, W. J. Cronyn, Matthew Thielen, Henry Smith 2d, George L. Brown, Tellico Johnson, M. G. Weber, Frank Hammond, Charles A. DeLaney, William M. Bloomer, Samuel Root, Charles R. FitzGerald, Henry G. Falke, Henry Schafer, James C. Holliday, J. N. Preston, George R. Wolfe, Arthur L. Knight, George Reimann, J. L. Whittet, Oren G. Nichols, Robert C. Titus, Andrew Shiels, Eugene S. Knapp, George L. Kingston, A. Oppenheimer, Louis P. Adolff, Jr., Charles J. Close, Albert F. Miller, J. H. Horton, George H. Clarke, Charles E. Markham, Will H. Dick, Clark W. Rice, George J. H. Goehler, Frank T. Haggerty, Robert T. Walker, Fred Wm. Fisher, W. H. Hoag, James L. Walker, George H. Young, E. E. Coatsworth, Henry G. Knapp, William J. Runcie, W. L. Alexander, W. H. Rice, James Chalmers, O. E. Goldhagen, John Malcolm and T. L. Wadsworth.

The Chapter was called to order by Prince John L. Brothers, who announced that the meeting had been called for the purpose of organizing Buffalo Chapter of Rose Croix, by the election of officers. Following the reading of the letters patent, naming the three leading officers under dispensation, an election was held, with the following result; George L. Kingston and Henry Smith 2d, acting as tellers:

REV. CHARLES ELBERT RHODES, 32°
MOST WISE MASTER OF BUFFALO CHAPTER OF ROSE CROIX,
LITERARY CRITIC OF THE CONSISTORY AND A
STAUNCH SUPPORTER OF THE RITE

ANCIENT ACCEPTED SCOTTISH RITE

John L. Brothers	*Most Wise Master*
Charles E. Hayes	*Senior Warden*
Joel H. Prescott	*Junior Warden*
Frank S. Coit	*Orator*
Samuel Root	*Treasurer*
T. L. Wadsworth	*Secretary*
Andrew Shiels	*Hospitaler*
William M. Bloomer	*Master of Ceremonies*
James A. Given	*Captain of the Guard*
John Malcolm	*Sentinel*

At the second meeting held on February 24, 1903, it was voted that the regular meetings of the Chapter be held on the third Friday of each month, in the Masonic Temple, and that the trustees of the four bodies be empowered to procure necessary paraphernalia for a proper presentation of the work of the degrees.

A Bright Beginning.

The early history of the Chapter was free from the drawbacks which marked the initial days of the Lodge and Council. From the start the attendance was good and the number of initiates encouraging. The degrees were put on in full ceremonial form and every indication pointed to a most successful future.

At the eighth regular assembly of Buffalo Chapter, the Charter granted by the Supreme Council under date of September 21, 1893, was duly received. On motion, it was resolved that the officers chosen at this Assembly, "shall hold their several offices until the regular annual meeting in 1895." On motion, it was resolved that the three principal officers named in the letters patent, be retained without ballot. An election was then held for the remaining officers resulting as follows:

Frank S. Coit, Orator; Samuel Root, Treasurer; T. L. Wadsworth, Secretary; Andrew Shiels, Hospitaler; Wm. M. Bloomer, Master of Ceremonies; James A. Given, Captain of the Guard; John Malcolm, Tiler, appointed. Choristers, Fred Erfling, William Page, James W. Chatman, Albert T. Brown.

Consistory Officers Received.

Officers of Buffalo Consistory were then received in full ceremonial form, and under direction of Ill. Charles W. Cushman, Commander-in-Chief, the first elected officers of Buffalo Chapter of Rose Croix were installed. That the first selection of officers had been wisely guided, is proven by the long period of service to which the presiding officer and his capable staff were called.

Practically no break in the official line occurred from the time of organization in 1893, until the election held on May 15, 1903, ten years. At that time, Ill. John L. Brothers was twice elected unanimously to the high office of Most Wise Master and was forced twice to decline, making it clear to the brethren that he could, under no circumstances, again accept the election or undertake the duties of the office. His retirement was felt to be a serious loss to the Chapter, in which he had been the same sustaining force that Ill. Brother Cushman had proven in the Consistory.

ANCIENT ACCEPTED SCOTTISH RITE

The decision of Ill. Brother Brothers resulted in the first real change in the official family. Charles E. Hayes was elected Most Wise Master, he having served as Senior Warden during the life of the Chapter. Harry W. Crabbs was chosen Senior Warden; William D. Cushman, Junior Warden; Edward K. Emory, Orator; William H. Bradish, Master of Ceremonies, and Walter M. Zink, Captain of the Guard, being appointed. At the meeting held on November 20, 1903, Prince Charles E. Hayes, Most Wise and Perfect Master elect, declined to be installed, explaining that he took such action, in order that Ill. John L. Brothers might be continued in the office. By unanimous vote it was ordered that the Secretary request a special dispensation from the Supreme Council, to hold an election to fill vacancies. As a result of the election which followed on December 18, 1903, Ill. John L. Brothers was again elected unanimously Most Wise Master, finally accepting under pressure of the members. He was re-elected in 1904 and again in 1905, but at this time positively declined to accept the office, expressing his appreciation of the great honor done him by his brethren, but showing clearly the impossibility of acceding to their wishes. As a result, Harry W. Crabbs was chosen Most Wise Master, William D. Cushman, Senior Warden; Edward K. Emory, Junior Warden; William H. Bradish, Orator; Walter M. Zink, Master of Ceremonies, and Hugh A. Sloan, Captain of the Guard. These officers were installed by Ill. Brother Brothers, with an impressiveness seldom equaled on a similar occasion.

At the election of 1906, the elective officers were returned, with the exception of William H. Bradish, the station of Orator being given to Walter M. Zink. Hugh A. Sloan was advanced to the office of Master of Ceremonies and Fred B. Griffith, Jr., was appointed Captain of the Guard.

Observant of Feast Days.

Buffalo Chapter of Rose Croix has been obediently observant of the established feast days, including Maundy Thursday, Easter, St. John's Day, and other significant occasions. On Thursday evening, March 28, 1907, the first observance of the Passover was publicly conducted. There was an elaborate program, of vocal and instrumental music, addresses, and the impressive ceremony of "extinguishing the lights," Fred B. Griffith, Jr., Hugh A. Sloan, Charles N. Armstrong, Walter M. Zink, Edward K. Emory, William D. Cushman and Harry W. Crabbs officiating. The feast of the Pascal Lamb followed. An equally impressive observance was held on the following Sunday, at a constitutional assembly of the Chapter, in commemoration of Easter. The ceremony of "relighting the lights" was performed. These observances have been annual events in the life of Buffalo Chapter of Rose Croix.

At the election held on May 17, 1907, William D. Cushman was elected Most Wise Master, Edward K. Emory, Senior Warden; Hugh A. Sloan, Junior Warden; Fred B. Griffith, Jr., Orator. Charles Elbert Rhodes was appointed Master of Ceremonies and H. Edson Webster, Guard. No change was made in the positions of Treasurer, Secretary or Tiler. These officers were returned at the succeeding election, May 15, 1908, although Fred B. Griffith, Jr., was elected Junior Warden and Charles Elbert Rhodes was chosen Orator, Coleman E. Byram being appointed Master of Ceremonies. No changes were made in the personnel of the officers in 1909, and they were again chosen in 1910, by unanimous vote. In 1911, owing to the departure of Brother William D. Cushman from the city, an advancement of the officers became imperative, though it was with regret that the brothers were obliged to dispense with the services of Brother Cushman, who by his zeal and loyalty to the craft, had, in a measure, made up to the fraternity something of the loss they had sustained in the passing of his Illustrious father. Hugh A. Sloan was elected Most Wise Master, and other officers all advanced one station, Henry B. Saunders being appointed Guard.

Present Official Family.

No change was made in the official line in 1912. Prosperity rested in generous measure upon the body, and harmony prevailed. The increase of membership continued most satisfactory. In 1913, as the custom had been established in Lodge and Council, there came an advancement of officers, Fred B. Griffith, Jr., being elected to succeed Sovereign Prince Sloan, and his associate officers progressing one step. The only addition to the line was Ill. Alan H. G. Hardwicke, as Master of Ceremonies, and William B. Frye, Guard. There was no change in 1914. A feature of Brother Griffith's administration was that each of the constitutional meetings were held as officially required.

As in the Council, so in the Chapter of Rose Croix, routine business marked the proceedings of 1915. There was no lessening of the activity which had characterized the several bodies for half a decade, the membership being increased in a satisfactory degree. There was no depreciation in the character of the exemplification of the beautiful Chapter degrees. At the election held on May 21, Frederick B. Griffith, Jr., retired as Most Wise Master, and the following officers were chosen for the ensuing year:

Charles Elbert Rhodes	*Most Wise Master*
H. Edson Webster	*Senior Warden*
Henry D. Saunders	*Junior Warden*
H. J. Emerson	*Orator*
Samuel Root	*Treasurer*
Harry D. Hosmer	*Secretary*
Walter M. Zink	*Master of Ceremonies*
Andrew Shiels	*Hospitaler*
Rev. Henry Ward	*Prelate*
Rev. James Cosbey	*Prelate*
George H. Clarke	*Sentinel*

The total membership on January 1, 1916, was 2697. There had been eighteen deaths for the last Masonic year, ten had demitted, and the total gain for the year had been 240.

CONSISTORY HOUSE

Real Home of Scottish Rite in the Valley of Buffalo—Its Purposes and Its Many Activities.

BUFFALO Consistory of the A. A. S. R., stands today as a signal triumph of the endeavors of devoted, zealous and loyal Scottish Rite Masons inspired by an ideal. These brethren of the craft have long shown and are still demonstrating the principles of brotherly love; of fraternity and Christian charity, upon which the oldest and greatest of secret societies was founded.

Situated at the entrance of the City's principal residence thoroughfare, the place of so large a portion of the refinement, religious activity and intellectual culture of the city, it has well been termed by one of the local newspapers, "the center of Buffalo's social activities," and as another has not inaptly observed, "the gateway to Delaware Avenue."

Approaching the spacious property from Niagara Square and the handsome McKinley monument, the visitor's first glance catches the imposing Cathedral with its sharply gabled roof and Heaven-pointing minarets, that time-honored edifice once dedicated to the service of God, as the "Church of Our Father," a most appropriate place for the teaching of those sacred truths of the Order, which nowhere are presented with greater impressiveness than by the earnest workers here.

While showing from the outside none of the extensive alterations and improvements made to its interior following its purchase by the Scottish Rite in 1905, there is still an impressive majesty, a sentimental imagery about the place, which takes a strong hold upon the observer who studies its graying walls for the first time. It is, to the members of the Rite, a loved shrine where, no matter what station in life a Brother may occupy, all "meet on the level and part on the square." Within its time-honored precincts many hundred Master Masons have been inducted into the mysteries of the Ineffable, Philosophical and Chivalric grades. Here they have learned that Masonic Brotherhood, in truth, makes no distinction of wealth or title; that the one principle of true manhood, reveals in this sanctuary, the correct solution of the problem: "Who is thy neighbor?"

A Gardener's Secret.

Passing from contemplation of the Cathedral, the visitor is surprised as his eyes rest upon the velvety carpet of green, broad in expanse as a park, an emerald setting for the Consistory House, the spacious Club which the Scottish Riters have made in fact a "Home," as the builder originally planned. A fine lawn it is; none fairer along the extended reach of Delaware Avenue, famous for its elegant frontal prospects. Many expressions of admiration have been heard and the inquiry has often been directed to Michael Knopf, care-taker, by what method he had secured such striking results in turf-growing.

"All one needs," replies Michael, "is a little hard work each day in each year, for thirty-six years."

Michael has been the care-taker of the place for just that period; for the former owner, Mr. Blocher, more than two decades, and for the Consistory since it came into possession of the fraternity.

The Consistory House, which was occupied as the private residence of the founder of the famous Blocher Home at Williamsville, was, in its original conception, a substantial structure, with spacious rooms, finished in costly woods and arranged for private convenience. This has been somewhat altered to meet the requirements of its present occupants, but none of its pristine elegance has been destroyed. That the home of the former philanthropist, whose later years were employed in a labor of love and service to his fellows, should have become the dwelling place of the great Scottish Rite body, whose charity is so conspicuous when known, yet so zealously guarded from public gaze, seems almost an inspirational development. The spirit of the one-time master of the handsome mansion—if those who have gone before can perceive and understand to what use their possessions here have been put—must feel a supreme satisfaction in that which has taken his place. In no corner of the earth is there more clearly typified that declaration of the Supreme Architect of the Universe, "Peace on Earth, Good Will to Men," than under the roof which houses the members of the Scottish Rite.

A Valued Souvenir.

Entering the wide doors, where to worthy Masons the latch-string ever hangs outward, we find ourselves in a spacious hall extending through the entire building. Rich rugs cover its floors and valuable paintings embellish the walls and gladden the eye. Near the entrance, appropriately framed, is an official copy of the resolutions adopted by the Supreme Council Sovereign Grand Inspectors General, of the 33d and last Degree, on the occasion of the meeting of the Supreme Council in annual session in the Valley of Buffalo, in September, 1908. It is an engrossed copy of the resolution, carrying the signatures of the Supreme officers, and was expressive of the appreciation of the grand body for the hospitable entertainment accorded them by the officers and members of Buffalo Consistory and co-ordinate bodies.

Passing to the basement first, we find nearly the entire space occupied by a convenient and artistic dining room, richly appointed, and capable of seating 250 guests. Here the simplest lunch, or the most elaborate meal, may be procured by the members, on order. Competent chefs are on duty, the cuisine is all that could be desired, the service admirable.

On the first floor, on either side of the great hall, are large, high-ceilinged rooms, which have been furnished by various Consistory classes. In the list of these contributors are the classes of 1907, 1912, 1913, 1914 and 1915. Each of these classes have furnished one room complete. Others have contributed to the adornment of both Consistory House and the Cathedral, by donations of expensive pieces of furniture or decoration. The class of 1915 was most liberal in its contribution to the adornment of the Consistory House. Not only is the furniture of its room rich and reposeful, but the crowning feature is a mammoth group picture of the class, the central figure of which is Illustrious Brother William Homan, 33° Active, Deputy for the State of New York, and a most loyal supporter of the Buffalo Body, for whom the class is named. Ill. Brother Homan was present, when the 250 worthy Princes were enlightened regarding the Royal Secret, and was sponsor for the class. Of these elegant rooms, two have been set aside for the special accommodation of ladies who visit the Consistory.

Women in a Masonic institution? Why, surely! Are not the Daughters of the American Revolution and the Colonial Dames, with kindred organizations, as welcome at Consistory House as the Sons? Patriotism and Masonry are synonymous here, and those who represent those principles are sure of a cordial welcome. In these rooms the wives, mothers, sisters and daughters of loyal Masons may meet, consult and become better acquainted, uniting with the brotherhood of man, the sisterhood of woman.

ALL PLEDGE FEALTY.

Another apartment is known as the Commander-in-Chief's room. Here distinguished fraternal guests are received, welcomed, and enlightened as to the purposes, accomplishments and ambitions of Buffalo Consistory. It is not too much to say that they speedily become enthusiasts and swear fealty to Ill. Brother Staples and his Consistory Army.

Then there is the Steward's room, where Brother Wellington Z. Jarden at present presides; a chess room and library in which Brother and Past Most Wise Master, Fred B. Griffith, Jr., marshals his forces for the ivory onslaught, and Brother Carl W. Knaus regales his adversaries with legends of knights and rooks. There is a smoking room in the rear of the Steward's apartment, which may, on occasion, serve for an executive meeting place, and a cloak room, convenient and commodious, two ideas which appear to have been paramount in the minds of the brothers who designed the arrangements of the place.

On the second floor are fitted up a lecture room, where frequent dissertations on seasonable topics are presented. Several committee rooms have frequent use by various societies, not united, yet allied with the Consistory organization. There are commodious offices, where the secular business of the Consistory is transacted; where the Commander-in-Chief consults with his officers, scrutinizes the bills presented; writes the checks to meet the expenses of a truly expansive corporation, and sends out his orders to his trusty staff. It requires close attention and a clear head, to direct the management of a business representing an investment of $250,000, in which something over 2,600 Brothers are stockholders, a truly substantial family.

Place for Recreation.

Recreation, is not overlooked, in the arrangement of Consistory House. On the third floor are found the billiard and pool tables, where friendly championship matches are played, by the more or less expert artists of the cue. There are, besides, many games of skill, for the pleasure and amusement of the members of the Consistory family. Thus the Consistory House has been converted into a real, a luxurious and a model Club. No gambling of any sort is permitted in any portion of the premises; intoxicating beverages are taboo; profanity and vulgarity are conspicuous by their total absence. There are all the advantages, with none of the objectionable features, of the average modern Club. The motto of Consistory House is: "Be a gentleman." It is the worked out principle taught by Ill. Charles W. Cushman, in the early days of the Buffalo Consistory organization.

The plumbing, electric lighting and other accessories are of the latest type. The atmosphere is home-like and comfortable. For all these comforts and advantages for improvement and entertainment, the members pay no assessments. Every Brother who meets the annual dues in Lodge, Council, Chapter and Consistory, receives a card with his receipt for the same, entitling him to all the privileges of the Club. No wonder the membership list is growing with astonishing rapidity. Man is a social animal, and in Consistory House real sociability, free from the grosser impulses, meets its full realization.

A Connecting Corridor.

In the earlier days of the Consistory, after it had removed from Masonic Temple, entrance to the Cathedral was had direct from the Avenue. With the acquisition of Consistory House, it was deemed expedient to connect the two buildings, and an arched corridor joins the Club, where social and intellectual pleasures hold sway, and the real work-shop of the order, where Masonic truths are revealed to the novice in ripest perfection. This corridor is carpeted, steam-heated and well lighted. It leads directly from the Steward's room. Members and visitors, under the existing arrangement, must first enter Consistory House, register and obtain a card, which admits them to the sacred precincts of the Cathedral.

In the Cathedral the arrangements are all that can be desired for the accommodation of the members; the preparation and introduction of the large classes, and the exemplification of the impressive and beautiful degrees of the order.

ANCIENT ACCEPTED SCOTTISH RITE

The stage is supplied with appropriate scenery and settings, its equipment being second in point of completeness and effectiveness, to none in the United States. The electrical appliances are the newest and best procurable. The Stage Director, Major George Metzger, and his corps of assistants, are well versed in their duties and attentive to them. The audience room has a seating capacity of several hundred, under the hanging drapery of the famous Consistory flags. The East, in Buffalo Cathedral auditorium, is striking in its conception and most appropriate. It is properly decorated with a beautiful depiction of the advent of light, represented by a sunburst, the great rays extending in every direction, projected from a central source. Upon this center rests the most important symbol of the Ancient Accepted Scottish Rite, the triangle supported upon the top of a double-headed eagle; within the triangle the figures 32; the eagle resting upon a sword, and below, the motto of the Thirty-second degree: *"Speas mea in deo est."* Between, and in the rays, are the three, five, seven and nine numbers of the Lodge of Perfection, represented by electric stars. Within the circle, a Teutonic cross shines forth, representing the Consistory when at work, and the sea of clouds, rolling back from the force of the rays of light, symbolizes the driving back of the powers of darkness by the force of Masonic light. Upon the lintel of the proscenium arch appears the Latin inscription: *"Ad Universi Terrarum Orbis Summi Architecti Gloriam."*

Frederick II, King of Prussia, was initiated into Free Masonry A. D. 1738, and from that date until 1747, was very active in the work of the craft. As a mark of respect and remembrance, the double-headed eagle was adopted, as the emblem of a Prince of the Royal Secret, as well as Inspector General, 33d and Last Degree, which Frederick for some time held, and to whom some historians have given credit for its institution.

ELABORATE WARDROBE.

In the rear of the stage, and in the spacious basement, is stored the elaborate wardrobe provided for the appropriate garbing of more than a thousand participants in the degree work. Nothing is lacking, from the sandal of the humblest peasant, to the royal robes of kings. Customs have been drawn upon, from all the nations of the earth, where Masonic light has penetrated. Suitable paraphernalia, and dress for each of the twenty-nine degrees exemplified in full form in Buffalo Consistory, is properly assorted and conveniently placed, at the disposition of the participants when needed. There are suitable and convenient dressing rooms for the officers of the various degrees. Everything is adjusted with an idea to promptness, effectiveness and correctness.

On the second floor is a large hall, which was originally used as a refrectory, but which today is utilized for drills, rehearsals and the like, by the various special organizations of the Consistory. It is decorated with portraits of all local

PROSCENIUM ARCH IN THE EAST OF BUFFALO CONSISTORY CATHEDRAL

33° Masons. Here the Consistory Band, the Grenadier Corps, the Drum Corps, the Turkish Band and the Saxophone Sextette hold their meetings, try out new effects, and fraternize with their fellows. This room is also used as a class room, when the Secretary's apartment adjoining, becomes over-crowded. Throughout, a perfect system is maintained, and there is no conflict of any sort among the large number of activities maintained. Lockers and uniforms are provided for individual members of all organizations sanctioned by the Consistory officers.

Seek Mental Improvement.

But this great organization has higher aims, more intense and laudible purpose, than the addition of names to its membership roll. Its officers have a fixed idea that social, mental, intellectual and fraternal improvement should go hand in hand. In furtherance of this idea, encouragement is given to all these special activities, and places for meetings are provided free, to all members who desire to avail themselves of the opportunity.

In educational features the Consistory has not been backward. The Literary Clinic has the use of a room once a month and the meetings are conducted with much interest and profit. The Ministers' Club meets here nearly every Monday. Each Friday noon, the Consistory Dinner Club has dinner in Consistory House, to be followed by an address by some prominent speaker or lecturer. Sometimes there are discussions on topics of general public interest, conducted in a spirit of friendliness and good-fellowship. There may be conflict of opinions and ideas, but differences never assume tangible form. The true purpose of these gatherings is intellectual betterment.

Musical And Dramatic.

In the membership of the Consistory there is a wealth of musical and dramatic talent, which is employed on frequent occasion for the benefit of the fraternity. Back in 1908, when the Supreme Council held its annual sessions in Buffalo, a production of the Holy City was proposed, as a means of providing a fund for the entertainment of the distinguished visitors. Ready response from the members followed the suggestion, and the dramatic representation was of a character to gain for the participants unstinted praise. By this entertainment was revealed to an extent the histrionic ability at the command of the Consistory, and since that time, many developments have been made in the line of dramatic, musical or literary entertainment.

Whether it is a reading by Brother Albert Zink, whose recent rendition of the "Melting Pot" by Zangwell, was highly approved by a large audience in the Cathedral auditorium; a burlesque or minstrel skit by the Entertainers, or the more classical program provided by the Consistory singers, the pleasure of the audience is assured. This talent is called into requisition on the occasion of the various holidays, the Washington, Lincoln and Independence Day anniversaries being observed by appropriate exercises, as well as the Christian festivals. At such times, special original features are introduced, which serve to emphasize the resourcefulness and constructive ability of the Entertainers. Walter Zink's "Qualities of Washington," written and delivered by that talented Brother for the special gratification of his fellow Consistory workers, is one of the finest tributes to the Father of His Country, given to the public. At these celebrations, members of the various local patriotic societies and the military are invited guests.

Fraternal Visits.

With all its home attractions, Buffalo Consistory has not lived entirely within itself. Its influence has radiated. Fraternal visits have been made to Moore Consistory at Hamilton, Ont., to Syracuse, Corning and Rochester Consistories. On each occasion the Buffalo brethren have exemplified degrees in full form for the benefit of their hosts and have been rewarded by the evident pleasure and appreciation of their audiences.

Whether Buffalo Consistory has been a strong factor in cementing more friendly relations with our neighbors to the North, is perhaps open to question, but certain it is, that the most fraternal feeling has been encouraged and maintained with the Scottish Rite bodies of the Dominion of Canada. Buffalo Consistory has had the honor and pleasure of welcoming some of the most distinguished government officials and members of the Rite in that country. A recent visitor to Consistory House was Ill. John Morrison Gibson, 33d Active, Lieutenant-Governor-General of the Dominion. Another frequent guest is Ill. Benjamin Allen 33°, Sovereign Grand Commander of the Supreme Council of Canada, coming here to meet and to greet, Ill. Barton Smith, 33°, of Toledo, Sovereign Grand Commander of the Supreme Council for the Northern Jurisdiction of the United States. When men of this stamp meet and clasp hands, in the confidence of fraternal brotherhood, the influence of the act, passing through and from them to the associate members of the order in the two countries, will reach further than one can conceive.

Masonic Charities.

With all its organization, social, intellectual and amusement activities, Buffalo Consistory does not overlook nor neglect worthy charity, though its philanthropy has never been exploited with the blare of publicity. Its work in the direction of relieving suffering and distress is conducted quietly and unostentatiously, in the true Christian spirit. Each Monday wives of Consistory members meet at Consistory House and sew for charity, making clothing for destitute children of the city. They work in co-operation with the Distrist Nurses Association, making personal investigation of cases to which their attention is directed. These devoted, unselfish women, shrink from publicity, seeking only relief of the distress of poverty and the approval of their own consciences. Keeping in touch with the physicians of the city, they are able to dispense their charity where it is most needed, and neglected babyhood has no more thoughtful friend, than the Consistory Sewing Circle.

CHARITABLE INNOVATIONS.

Equally active in caring for members of the Craft, who have met with misfortune or become ill or stranded in our city, are the officers of the Consistory. An understanding is had with all public officials, the police and hotels, by which cases of distress among the brethren are at once reported, investigation made, and assistance rendered, in legitimate channels. While the charity of Consistory House is broad, it is never dispensed in a haphazard or random manner. No deserved help is denied; no unworthy applicant is recognized. Not only are the principles of true Christian charity maintained by the Consistory, but encouragement is given to the work of organized charitable institutions. Use of the Consistory buildings is freely contributed to this end, church and philanthropical societies being given a hearty welcome. Many innovations have been introduced by the present Commander-in-Chief, calculated to bring happiness and cheer to the city's suffering and needy. Each Christmas for the past four years, the Crippled Children and the Wheel-Chair Children have enjoyed a mammoth Christmas tree, in the auditorium of the Cathedral. Officers and members have contributed in gifts and labor, to make these occasions all that they should be, to brighten the lives of the unfortunate little ones with the real spirit of Christmas. Yet so quietly and undemonstratively are all these good works conducted, that many members of the organization will learn from these pages, for the first time, the full scope of Consistory endeavor.

Bodies Well Officered.

Buffalo Consistory and co-ordinate bodies have been particularly fortunate in the selection of their officers, not only in the early days of the organization, but in recent times. Especially is this true of the two principal bodies, Palmoni Lodge and Buffalo Consistory, in which practically all of the business interests of the Scottish Rite in the Valley of Buffalo are centered. By a provision of the constitution, all financial questions are considered and acted upon in Palmoni Lodge, after reference to the associate bodies.

The present Thrice Potent Master, Brother Charles I. Heckman, is not only a capable and careful business man, but no member of Buffalo Consistory holds a higher appreciation of Masonic work, or could be more earnest in helping to promote its principles. An indefatigable worker; with the complete ritual of the degrees conferred in the various bodies carried constantly in his mind; a great stickler for accuracy in rendition, determined at all times to bring out every detail which will add to the attractiveness, impressiveness and perfection of the work, he is a valuable aid to the Commander-in-Chief and a striking example of force, efficiency and zeal.

BLUE LODGE MASONRY.

Brother Heckman is active in Blue Lodge Masonry, having been instrumental in the organization of Tyrian Lodge, and its first Worshipful Master. The rapid growth and excellent work of that Lodge is strong proof of Brother Heckman's sincerity in his Masonic adherence and his loyalty to the craft.

This dual connection with Symbolic Masonry and the Ineffable degrees of the Scottish Rite, are of importance, as demonstrating the gradual but effective removal of the barriers which, though really imaginary, still in the earlier days, served to interfere with that harmony which should always exist between all branches of the Craft. All brethren of legitimate Masonry should go hand in hand, working in complete accord, whether their fraternal home may be in the Chapter, Council or Commandery of the York Rite, or the more detailed and equally impressive grades of the Scottish Rite. Gradually, but certainly, that desired consummation is being brought about, and all misunderstandings, diverse ambitions and rivalries, will soon become a thing of the past. Cemented in the bonds of a true and harmonious brotherhood, Masonry will endure through all the coming ages. It is the workers in the craft and the exemplars of the true Masonic principles, like Brother Heckman and his associate officers, who are doing much toward the attainment of this desirable end.

Chief Directing Force.

Ill. George K. Staples, 33°, Commander-in-Chief of Buffalo Consistory, and the directing force of the Rite in the Valley of Buffalo, has demonstrated in many ways his particular fitness for the important and laborious duties which the office imposes. Ill. Brother Staples has been an originator as well as an executive, and his fertile brain has constantly been active in devising added means and methods for the stimulation of interest among the members, as well as to the formation of a complete and smoothly working business organization. He was largely instrumental in adding the Blocher property to the Consistory real estate holdings, and it has been due principally to his initiative and good judgment, backed by an indomitable will and tireless energy, which has given to the members the model Club rooms and the diversified activities which have served to make it famous, as a social and fraternal center.

Whatever of opposition has appeared, has, by its unreasonableness, served simply to strengthen the regard of the members of Buffalo Consistory and make them more determined to give their loyal support to a Commander, whose heart and soul are in the work given into his hands. No more striking proof of the efficiency displayed by Ill. Brother Staples can be had, than the appreciation felt for his accomplishments by the members of

ENTRANCE AND SECTION OF MAIN HALL IN CONSISTORY HOUSE

the Supreme Council, Sovereign Grand Inspectors General, of the 33d and Last Degree. The approval of the progress made by Buffalo Consistory under his leadership, from Ill. Brother William Homan, Deputy of the Supreme Council for the State of New York, is above the influence of jealous rivalry or the misrepresentation of slanderous tongues.

TIME AND ENERGY.

During his incumbency of the high and responsible position of Commander-in-Chief, Ill. Brother Staples has contributed lavishly of his time and energy to place Buffalo Consistory in the very front rank of Scottish Rite organizations in the United States. He has seen, and been quick to grasp, the opportunity to build up a powerful organization, the influence of which should be strongly felt, not alone in fraternal circles, but in the social, civic and professional activities of the municipality. It was his idea that Masonry meant more than the perfunctory dissemination of ritualistic teachings, or the imparting of those mysterious secrets which afford food for wild conjecture in the minds of the layman. He realized that in order to hold this great army of brethren to their duties and their faith, it was necessary to provide those essentials of amusement, recreation and interest, which men in every station and of every degree, crave and require. Three important steps were necessary for such a development.

First, the acquisition of suitable quarters where the brethren could meet and fraternize, not so much as Masons, but as friends, loyal and true. The Blocher property with its spacious mansion and expansive grounds, immediately adjoining the Cathedral, afforded the legitimate means for the accomplishment of the first step. At first glance, to less ambitious members of the Rite, the purchase of this valuable property appeared a great risk and pessimistic brethren predicted failure and counseled delay. But the spirit of enthusiasm, stimulated by the optimism of the Staples type, gained the day, and the desirable property was acquired. Then came the alteration and furnishing of the Consistory House, to meet the needs of the prospective occupants and make it commensurate with the requirements of a modern Club. That too, was readily accomplished under the inspiring energy of the Commander-in-Chief and his loyal lieutenants, and through the appreciation of the members of the various classes expressed in generous contributions, for the garnishing of the beautiful rooms. Then came the third step—the encouragement to organization of various activities among the members, directed to the social, musical, literary and scientific interest of those who might come to the Consistory House, either as regular habitues, or occasional visitors. That also has been accomplished, and today Buffalo Consistory affords greater and more varied attractions to its members and friends, than any social or professional Club in the City.

Financial results in connection with the operations of the Consistory have been satisfactory.

Many thousands of dollars have been expended in providing an equipment, in both Cathedral and Consistory House, commensurate with the large membership and the proper exemplification of the work of the Rite. Constant additions are being made to the wardrobe and paraphernalia, for completeness in every detail, is a fad if it may be so termed, with the directing head of the organization. Yet for all this needful though expensive outlay, the debts of the Consistory are being satisfactorily reduced. Some idea of the magnitude of the financial responsibilities of the Scottish Rite in this city and the extent of its resources, may be drawn from the last report of the Trustees, presented at the annual reunion and covering the amount of property in their hands on June 1, 1915, as follows:

REPORT OF TRUSTEES

June 1, 1915.

Real Estate.

Cathedral	$109,663.98
Consistory House	104,882.56
Increase	4,077.89

Total	$218,624.43
Mortgages	$ 89,400.00
Equity	129,224.43
	$218,624.43

PARAPHERNALIA AND PERSONAL PROPERTY.

June 1, 1914............$ 19,078.00
Increase 18,051.88

Total (Inventory)...$ 37,129.88

RECAPITULATION.

Real estate $218,624.43
Paraphernalia, etc. 37,129.88
Trustee's bank account (gifts).......   169.00

Total assets $255,923.31

Respectfully submitted,
GEORGE K. STAPLES, 33°
FRANKLIN E. BARD, 32°
Trustees.

SECRETARY'S REPORT.

From the Secretary's report we find that the receipts from all sources for the fiscal year, were $60,150.91, and the disbursements $54,313.66, leaving a balance on hand June 1, 1915, of $5,837.25. Of the disbursements, $2,788.69, was paid in taxes; $2,545 for Supreme Council dues and $1,846.96 for additional costumes. The disbursements of 1914-15, include practically all of the alteration and equipment of Consistory House. In the report of the Finance Committee, which is composed of Ill. William H. Ellis, Brother David C. Howard and Brother George A. Keller, it is stated:

"Your committee takes pleasure in reporting that it has carefully examined the annual reports of the Secretary and of the Treasurer, together with their books and vouchers, and finds them correct in every particular. In our judgment, the system in vogue throws every safeguard about the funds of the Consistory, and we are satisfied that they have been fully and duly accounted for."

Cradle And The Grave.

Ill. Brother Staples believes, with the Psalmist, that there is "a time to work and a time to dance; a time to be merry and a time for sorrow." In Buffalo Consistory the members have gathered in honor of a new life, and to pay their last tribute to a departing Brother. Christenings and funerals have taken place in the Cathedral auditorium; honors have been paid to the cradle and the grave. Marriage vows have here been plighted. Devotees of Terpsichore among the brethren, with their ladies, have tripped the light fantastic to the music of the Consistory orchestra, on frequent occasions. Dinner parties, receptions, lectures and entertainments have served to please, instruct and amuse the thousands of members and visitors who have enjoyed the hospitality of Consistory House, during the past three years. There is a spirit of freedom and good-fellowship about the place which gives it a remarkable charm, yet at all times the greatest decorum is preserved.

An Efficient Officer.

As chairman of the House Committee, Colonel George J. Haffa is the right man in the right place. With his efficient assistants, no feature calculated to impress or please the visitor, is overlooked. His affable manner is, in itself, a welcome and an assurance to those who enter the doors of Consistory House for the first time. No needful attention is forgotten, no courtesy is lacking. Colonel Haffa's selection for the delicate and responsible position is another evidence of the discernment and ability for organization of the Commander-in-Chief. Adding to a geniality and attractiveness of manner which win confidence, Chairman Haffa's long military experience has invested him with a disciplinary force which commands respect and obedience, and the affairs of Consistory House are conducted under his watchful eye, with propriety and above criticism.

But in all the enthusiasm of social pleasures, the more serious features of Masonic brotherhood, are not overlooked. Rigid observance of the constitutional meetings is required, and on these occasions, elaborate and appropriate programmes are carried out. St. John the Baptist's Day; Thanksgiving; Christmas; St. John the Evangelist's Day; Maundy Thursday, Easter, Ascension Day and Whitsunday are all religiously celebrated. During each year numerous visits are paid by the brethren in a body to some church, where special sermons for their delectation are preached by the pastors. Christian duty is not forgotten in the desire for Masonic extension.

Every heart-beat of the Consistory is a throb of patriotism. Flag Day, Lincoln's Birthday, Independence Day and Washington's Birthday, are occasions for renewed devotion to the principles of a free government and to the starry banner which each day in the year, floats proudly from the stately flag-pole in front of the Consistory entrance.

Encouraging Words.

Every notice of the monthly meetings, going out from Consistory House, carries some word of encouragement and suggestion from the Commander-in-Chief. Here is an example:

"The work of another year has begun. The success of Buffalo Consistory will depend upon the interest, attention, zeal and enthusiasm of the membership. Every worthy Mason should aspire to this closer followship. Numerical strength is not desired for the sake of members, but from the sure knowledge that the larger the number of men working in a common cause, the greater the sum total of good will be accomplished. Masonry, in general, is doing a great work and is teaching thousands of men how to live. When you have come to feel, to believe, to know that Scottish Rite Masonry in the Valley of Buffalo, gives to you greater opportunities for doing good, for self-development, for service to mankind, and, at the same time, gives to your families the privileges of a "Club," lectures, plays, musicals, dining service, in fact every social service, and all within the reach of the most humble Mason, you must then have an abiding interest, a close attention, a fervent zeal and a strong enthusiasm, for the wonderful work which is being done by Buffalo Consistory."

Symbolic Masonry.

Interest in Blue Lodge, or symbolic Masonry, is a characteristic of Buffalo Consistory, as has been noted heretofore. During the past few years the bonds of sympathy between the two organizations have constantly been strengthened. Following the organization of Charles W. Cushman Lodge No. 879, through the initiative and energy of Brother James L. Nixon, present Sovereign Prince of Palmoni Council, Brother Charles I. Heckman interested himself along similar lines, with the result that Tyrian Lodge, No. 925, was organized, with a large charter list of active and representative citizens.

On Saturday evening, May 29, 1915, Tyrian Lodge was consecrated, dedicated and constituted in the Buffalo Consistory Cathedral, by the Grand Master of Masons in the State of New York, Most Worshipful George Freifeld. It is doubtful if ever before, a similar ceremony was conducted in the auditorium of a Scottish Rite body. Ill. George K. Staples was selected as the first Senior Deacon of this lodge, and was duly installed, but owing to the demands made upon his time as head of the Consistory, was compelled to relinquish the office.

Another earnest Consistory worker, who has made a record for efficiency as a Council presiding officer; who has rendered valuable and commendable service by assuming innumerable difficult roles in the work of the various degrees of all the Scottish Rite bodies, has consented to take his place in the line of officers of Washington Lodge, No. 240, F. & A. M., having been appointed Senior Steward. It is characteristic of Brother Walter

BUFFALO CATHEDRAL AUDITORIUM

M. Zink, that whatever he undertakes is marked by a conscientious zeal and loyalty, and his services in Washington Lodge, no matter what the duties required, will be energetically and painstakingly rendered. The Master is to be congratulated on his good fortune in securing Brother Zink as a member of his official family.

SUPREME COUNCIL'S VISITS
Serve to Bring Consistory and Highest Body of the Scottish Rite Into Closer Relation.

IN 1895, the Supreme Council of Sovereign Grand Inspectors General made its first visit to Buffalo and the event was one of encouraging influence to Buffalo Consistory and co-ordinate bodies. Thirteen years later, in 1908, a second visit for the sessions of the Supreme Council, gave the members of that august body opportunity to observe the wonderful progress made by the Scottish Rite in the Valley of Buffalo. Long before the date of the annual meeting, active preparations were under way by the local Consistory, for the proper recognition, reception and entertainment of the distinguished guests. Committees were appointed and an elaborate program of entertainment planned. As a means of providing the necessary fund with which to meet the expenses of the reception proposed, a production by Consistory talent of the Christian drama, "The Holy City," was determined upon, and the best talent of the four bodies was drawn upon to take the various roles.

In the presentation which took place for five evenings of a week at the Cathedral, the following Consistory members, who had on frequent occasions demonstrated their dramatic ability, were assigned to the principal male characters: Barrabas, Brother Howard D. Herr; Judas, Ill. William L. Alexander; Caiaphas, Brother Albert H. Zink; Zacharias, Brother Charles S. Butler; Haabakuk, Brother Hugh A. Sloan; John, Brother Charles I. Heckman; Peter, Brother Fred B. Griffith, Jr.; Pilate, Brother Charles W. Mann; Silenus and the Centurion, Brother John S. Embleton; Micha, Brother Walter M. Zink; Lazarus, the Rev. Brother Coleman E. Byram. Many other members were as loyal and energetic in their supernumerary parts, as Roman citizens and Jewish peasants, as those who assumed the heavier roles. The ladies of the several Eastern Star Chapters co-operated generously by serving as ushers at each evening's performance, and in the female characters of the drama, Mrs. Helen Kingston, of Naomi Chapter, taking the difficult part of Mary Magdalen. The time and energy given by the members to a complete and entirely commendable presentation of the drama, was an example of the loyalty held by them for their beloved Consistory and the craft. Large and appreciative audiences greeted each performance and the financial results were eminently satisfactory. Later the drama was presented at the Star Theatre for two nights, with equally pleasing results.

EFFORTS APPRECIATED.

That the efforts of the Buffalo brethren to extend to their distinguished visitors a suitable welcome and to make their stay in the Valley of Buffalo a pleasurable period in their Masonic lives, were successful, was shown by the enthusiasm with which the officials and honorary members of the Supreme Body entered into the spirit of the program of entertainment provided. Lake, river and inland excursions were of daily occurrence, and the guests of Buffalo Consistory were unanimous and lavish in their expressions of praise. To many of them their introduction to the "Gateway to the Lakes" was a decided revelation. Never having visited Buffalo, the extent of the city's industries, its business activities; its cosmopolitan population and its wonderful importance as a connecting link between the water and rail facilities of the Northern Jurisdiction, gave them new and unexpected impressions of the magnitude of our resources and the spirit of progress dominating the municipality. To those interesting disclosures was added a realization of the expansion of the Scottish Rite in this Orient, which could not fail to give them appreciative pleasure. At the same time, the visit of the Supreme Council served as a stimulant to the brethren of the craft in this jurisdiction, and was to some degree responsible for the increased and constant activity which has characterized the Buffalo bodies of the Rite, since that time.

Unusual Testimonial.

An unusual and flattering testimonial, not alone of the progressiveness and attraction of Buffalo, but of the hospitable character of Buffalo Consistory, was that which came from the Supreme Council. At the closing session, the following preamble and resolution, by Ill. Brother Charles Theodore Gallagher, 33° Active, was presented and adopted unanimously:

"Adopting the suggestion of our always thoughtful and appreciative Sovereign Grand Commander, made to me within the hour, I arise for the purpose of placing upon our record an expression of the appreciation we feel of what has been done for us by the brothers of Buffalo Consistory during our all-too-short stay with them; with the memories of Niagara, its falls and gorge, as seen last evening by sunset and moonrise, mingled with the mist and roar of the torrent, an appropriate setting for the whole gem being the trolley ride with the banquet at the Clifton, it seems half a sin to try to put in words what one feels, at so delightful an entertainment, so hospitably presented on every hand. To those of us whose acquaintance with this beautiful city has been limited to a hasty transition in the train-sheds as one has passed East or West, the evidence of development and growth have opened our eyes with wonder, and the visit has been to us a mine of pleasure and delight.

Numerous Activities.

"Prosperity, mingled with the historic, the commercial and the artistic, is met with on every hand, presenting scenes that improve the mind, quicken the intellect and gladden the eye. Your public buildings and your commercial structures sustained by private enterprise, unsurpassed by any city of its size in the country, is each in itself a monument to the public spirit and civic pride of your citizens; your system of stock-yards and grain elevators is second to none in this great land teeming with the product of the farm and of the soil. Institutions of learning, of literature, of history and of art, each in a flourishing state, patronized by appreciative members, evidence the taste of your people; a system of parks covering more than a thousand acres, embellished by the skill of the landscape architect, in close proximity to the crowded portion of your city, affording breathing space and recreation to your half-million residents, reached by drives through avenues and boulevards lined with comfortable homes and costly residences, sustaining the reputation of your city for the highest ideals of municipal comfort and health, where more than fifty per cent. of your people own their own homes; your street system nearly three hundred miles in extent, with more miles of asphalt and smooth pavement than London, Paris or New York, broken at convenient intervals by historic squares containing public monuments not too numerous but all appropriate and artistic, demonstrates the hand of a genius in the art of engineering skill.

"In passing between the headquarters of our Supreme Council and the Consistory of your Cathedral, we have by one route, daily seen that attractive square, the terminal of your great interurban railway, named for that patriot of foreign birth who was the last of Washington's generals to receive his degrees as a Mason; while by the other route we have passed through that circle bearing the name of your neighboring eighth wonder of the world, adorned with that beautiful obelisk, white in its purity, pointing pathetically toward Heaven, placed there as a perpetual remembrance of that sainted man who lost his life in your midst, a beautiful tribute to our beloved President McKinley; the manner of whose death by the hand of a foreign fanatic was similar to that of the death of that other martyr, known to history as "William the Silent," of whom it was said as of our martyred President: "He lived the faithful rules of a brave people and when he died, children cried in the streets." By your kindness it has been possible and has been our good fortune to enjoy all these beauties and benefits.

Hospitality Appreciated.

"But if the senses have been delighted by what we have seen of your city, what shall I say in this presence, under this chronological order of banners, showing the evolution of our glorious flag, an illustrated description of which each of us bears away to his home as memory of our proceedings within these walls? What shall I say to the brethren of Buffalo Consistory who have labored so incessantly before their welcome on our arrival, until our final departure, to make an entertainment so enjoyable? The names of Judge Titus, Joel Prescott, William Lyons and Colonel Ward will ever be remembered by each of us, as the embodiment and representative of that larger body of Illustrious Brethren, who have given their time and means for our delectation. Our hearts are too full of appreciative kindness to attempt to state what we feel, but for the members of the Supreme Council and in their behalf, I will simply express our warmest gratitude and praise for the many courtesies extended; and for the purpose of making a record of what we feel toward our Buffalo brethren as hosts, the following is prepared that it may be entered upon our minutes and a copy, suitably engrossed, presented to the Buffalo Consistory of our Rite:

" 'Appreciating the untiring efforts of the brethren of Buffalo Consistory in their zeal to make the sojourn of their visitors a delightful entertainment, the members of the Supreme Council express their warmest feelings of gratitude and thanks for the cordial hospitality and many courtesies extended to them and to their ladies during their too brief stay in this prosperous and beautiful city; and as we regretfully part with our hosts, we extend to them our sincere wishes for a continuance of the prosperity and happiness that it has been their good fortune to enjoy.

"That this minute of our feelings may assume permanent form, an engrossed copy of the same, as extended on the records of our Council, shall be forwarded to Buffalo Consistory of our Rite.' "

The above resolution, beautifully engrossed, and signed by the Supreme Council officers, was, as has been previously stated, framed and given a place of honor in the Consistory House. It will ever be treasured by the members as a memento of one of the most important, as it was one of the most enjoyable events, in its history.

COUNCIL OF DELIBERATION

Visits to Buffalo Have Been Occasions of Much Interest—Full Appreciation Shown by the Distinguished Visitors.

IN chronicling the activities of Buffalo Consistory, some attention must be given to the reception accorded the members of the Council of Deliberation for the Bodies of the Ancient Accepted Scottish Rite, of the State of New York, of which Ill. William Homan, 33°, Active, Deputy for that state for the Supreme Council, is the Commander-in-Chief. Annual session of the Council of Deliberation was held in Buffalo in 1908, and again in 1913. At this later session, the visiting Supreme Officers were made more fully to realize the advancement which had been made in the Buffalo bodies and their expressions of approval were hearty and copious. At the last session, that of 1913, a cordial welcome was extended to the members of the Council by Ill. George K. Staples, Commander-in-Chief of Buffalo Consistory, on behalf of the Scottish Rite in the Valley of Buffalo, in the following words:

"Most Ill. William Homan, 33°, Commander-in-Chief of the Council of Deliberation for the State of New York, and representatives from the various Lodges, Councils, Chapters and Consistories, the co-ordinate Bodies of the Rite in the Valley of Buffalo bid you a hearty welcome, not only to

Buffalo Consistory, but to the City of Buffalo, the Queen City of the Lakes. We appreciate the great honor done us by selecting our home as the place for the 44th annual Convocation of the Council of Deliberation. We shall profit by your presence and from your Councils, and we shall get a new inspiration from you to go on and on, teaching men by our lives and our works, how to live in the spirit of Brotherly Love, actually recognizing that all men are our Brothers, and that all things belong to God.

Reached Majority.

"Notwithstanding that Buffalo Consistory is the youngest Consistory in the State of New York, we have reached our majority, and we renew our fealty to the Supreme Council and avow our loyalty to our Illustrious Deputy, and extend the right hand of fellowship to every Brother of the Rite.

"Welcome, thrice welcome, to you all—whatever we have is yours. Welcome, Welcome, Welcome, Brothers.

"The words of cheer, the helpful suggestion, the gentle reprimand, the stern direction—whatever you do or say—will be received by us as the caress, the advice, the reproof, the command of a loving parent to a dutiful child.

"May our conduct, each to the other, be in the spirit of Brotherly Love, and may it always stand the tests of justice, truth and toleration."

O, Spirit of Love, abide with us all;
  Give love and good cheer to lead us aright;
To work for the truth, respond to the call;
  Enlist in our ranks all men who seek light.

ANCIENT ACCEPTED SCOTTISH RITE

Our mission is Life, our trust is in God;
  Mankind is our field, on high is our aim;
To work and to strive; to strive and to plod;
  Reward will be sure, and Peace be our gain.

Illustrious Sirs, we greet you today;
  To you do we look, from you we demand
The brightest and best. The best, do we say?
  Then ours shall be yours, and yours to command.

We welcome you all to Lake Erie's shore,
  Where cool is the breeze, and warm is the heart;
We love you so well, your virtues adore,
  Our only regret you soon must depart.

Jewels Are Presented.

Ill. Arthur MacArthur, 33d, Active Member of the Supreme Council, responded to Ill. Brother Staples's welcome, for the Council of Deliberation, in an eloquent and fitting manner, paying a glowing tribute to the members of the Rite in the Valley of Buffalo, for their splendid achievements and progressiveness.

Ill. Robert C. Titus, 33°, on behalf of Buffalo Consistory, presented to the Council of Deliberation a complete set of jewels for its officers, and the same were accepted for the Council, by Most Illustrious William Homan, 33d Active, Commander-in-Chief, who appointed Buffalo Consistory the permanent custodian of the Jewels.

In the appointment of committees, the following members of Buffalo Consistory, were honored by the Commander-in-Chief: State of the Rite,

Hugh A. Sloan, Past Master Buffalo Chapter, Ill. William L. Alexander, Buffalo Consistory. Finance: Ill. George K. Staples, Commander Buffalo Consistory. General regulations: Ill. Robert C. Titus, Active Member Supreme Council, Wilbur H. Funk, Junior Warden Palmoni Council. Applications for new bodies: Walter F. Gibson, Master Palmoni Lodge, William H. Ellis, Past Sovereign Prince Palmoni Council. Place of Meeting: Ill. Samuel Root, Buffalo Consistory, Ill. Martin H. Blecher, Past Master Palmoni Lodge. Jurisprudence, Ill. Joel H. Prescott, Buffalo Consistory. Grievances: Charles I. Heckman, Deputy Master Palmoni Lodge, Ill. Morris Benson, Past Master Palmoni Lodge, Walter M. Zink, Past Sovereign Prince Palmoni Council. Antiquities: Charles W. Mann, Past Master Palmoni Lodge, Albert H. Zink, Past Sovereign Prince Palmoni Council. Deceased members: Ill. Francis T. Coppins, Buffalo Consistory, Rev. Carl D. Case, Grand Prior New York Council of Deliberation, Charles Elbert Rhodes, Senior Warden Buffalo Chapter of Rose Croix. Spurious and clandestine bodies: Fred B. Griffith, Jr., Master Buffalo Chapter of Rose Croix. Special committee on telegrams, Byron B. Daggett, Sovereign Prince Palmoni Council, Charles H. Andrews, Grand Captain of the Guard of the Council of Deliberation, George H. Clarke, Grand Sentinel. Special committee on Deputy's address, Ill. George L. Brown, James L. Nixon, High Priest, Palmoni Council.

ANCIENT ACCEPTED SCOTTISH RITE

In his annual address, Ill. Brother Homan, spoke enthusiastically of the work of the Buffalo bodies, commending them for the energy displayed and predicting continued prosperity. At the opening he said:

"Buffalo Consistory is just rounding out the twentieth year of its existence. It is the youngest Consistory in the State of New York, and at the time that the late lamented Charles W. Cushman, 33°, made application for the granting of their charter, doubt was expressed in some quarters throughout the State, of the necessity of a Consistory in Buffalo, and some fear was mingled with the doubt, that the Masonic population of this part of the State, was not sufficient to insure the permanence and stability of a Consistory. The Valley of Buffalo has been singularly fortunate in the development of men possessing great executive ability, earnestness and zeal, which have resulted in a phenomenal development of the Scottish Rite in and about Buffalo, during the last twenty years, so that at the present time, the membership in Buffalo Consistory is the second largest in the State of New York."

COMMITTEE COMMENDS.

The Committee on the State of the Rite, in its report, said:

"The report to the Committee on the State of the Rite, was one of the most extensive, and elaborate, that this Committee has ever received. Comprehensive, and yet bristling with details and information. It would seem as if the Scottish Rite Brethren of Buffalo were lying awake nights, thinking of something to do, novel and new. Thinking of days and events to celebrate, and ceremonies and observances, to be performed. The Committee on the State of the Rite most sincerely congratulate the Brethren of the Rite in the City of Buffalo, and we say to the Rite thoughout the State, that what can be done here in Buffalo, can be done elsewhere, and our advice is: 'Go and do likewise,' and the fruit of the vintage will make glad the hearts of the chroniclers.

"It was our good fortune to be invited by the Brethren of Buffalo Consistory to convene in annual Council of Deliberation in this city, in 1908, and the pleasant recollections of that meeting, still linger in our memories. During the last five years many changes have taken place in the personnel of the presiding officers in the Buffalo bodies, but the same spirit of hospitality prevails, and we find ourselves today, the welcome guests of Buffalo Consistory, under the auspices of the 44th annual convocation of the Council of Deliberation for the State of New York:"

His Warning Words

Ill. Brother Homan, further expressed his pleasure in the following:

"While discussing the preliminaries and the program to cover this occasion, it was necessary for me frequently to remind your large-hearted Commander-in-Chief, of the necessity of limiting your hospitality within proper bounds of economy, for it is our intention to discourage anything in the way of extravagant expenditures for hospitality, so that we may encourage humbler bodies of the Rite throughout the State, to invite us to convene with them, whenever they think it will be to their advantage to have us as their guests. Our hearts swell in grateful praise to the Grand Architect of the Universe, for having preserved so large a number of the representatives of the Scottish Rite to find it possible to favor us with their presence, and to lend their judgment and counsel to our deliberations. All the teachings of our beloved Rite are calculated to encourage all that is good in our natures, and to develop the true type of mankind.''

CONSISTORY CEREMONY OF BAPTISM.

An event of significance in Buffalo Consistory, one which was really an innovation in the Scottish Rite bodies in this section of the State, was the Masonic baptism, on June 1, 1913, of Ruth Katherine Daggett, infant daughter of Brother Byron B. Daggett, at that time Sovereign Prince of Palmoni Council. Masonic baptism is an ancient custom of the Rite, descending to us by legitimate transmission. It was formerly administered as a protective rite to the children of brethren of the Lodges of Perfection. It is a beautiful and dignified ceremony, and places the child forever under the careful guardianship of the Fraternity, wheresoever dispensed around the world. Any Brother of the Rite can request this privilege of his Lodge of Perfection, and it is in the province of the Lodge, to whom the request is made, to confer it. Brother Daggett made his request to Palmoni Lodge, Ill. George K. Staples, 33°, Commander-in-Chief of Buffalo Consistory, to act as Godfather, and Mrs. John Miller Horton, of the Daughters of the American Revolution, to act as Godmother. Of the several Past Thrice Potent Masters of Palmoni Lodge, Ill. Charles W. Mann was selected to prepare and present the ceremony, with the assistance of the officers of Palmoni Lodge of Perfection, and on Sunday afternoon, June 1, at 3 o'clock, for the first time in the history of the Rite in the Valley of Buffalo, the rite was administered with the following program:

Organ prelude.

Solo, "All Hail to the Morning."

Grand processional entrance, in following order: Captain of the Guard; Master of Ceremonies with Nine Brethren of the Lodge, who take vow with officers, father, mother and Godmother; Officers of Lodge in reverse order; Thrice Potent Master, the celebrant; Sovereign Princes.

Prayer by the Orator.

Hymn, "Old Hundred," by audience.

Opening of Lodge of Perfection in form by officers.

Entrance of parents with child and escort.

Ceremony of Baptism.

Choral solo.

Address.

Organ prayer, closing Lodge.

ALBERT H. ZINK, 32°
PAST SOVEREIGN PRINCE OF PALMONI COUNCIL PRINCES OF JERUSALEM, AND A CAPABLE AND VERSATILE DEGREE WORKER

ALBERT H. ZINK, 32°

Past Sovereign Prince, Palmoni Council, Whose Work in All The Bodies Deserves Praise.

BUFFALO Consistory has a small army of conscientious workers, who have displayed genuine talent, in stage representation and floor work. To particularize, by giving special praise or commendation to certain individuals, would be unjust to others, who, while perhaps not acting in stellar roles, are still necessary and invaluable, as component parts of the complete organization. No machine is stronger than its weakest part, and it is only with the assistance of the supernumeraries, that the principal artists are able to bring their representations to perfection.

There is no lack of dramatic talent in Buffalo Consistory. Absence of any slated participant in the work, no matter how important the role he is expected to assume, while it may weaken, cannot destroy the effectiveness of the result. Officers and members who are called upon to assist, have pride in their work and there is a constant endeavor for improvement. It is this ambition and energy which has served to place the Buffalo bodies of the Scottish Rite in the very front rank of the exemplars of the impressive degrees of the order, whether it be in the Ineffable, Historical,

Philosophical or Chivalric grades. Acolyte or King; Guard or Noble, there is the same marked earnestness, the same ambition and idealistic effort, inspired by a love of the Rite and a desire to display its principles more clearly to the mind of the candidate; to give its teachings more lasting imprint upon their hearts.

Without Discrimination.

But while it would be obviously unfair to discriminate, as to ability or resourcefulness, there is one member of the Consistory working force whose talents are of such high order; whose versatility is so great and whose personality takes such a firm hold upon the hearts of his brethren, that failure to extend to him a meed of special commendation, would be regarded by the members as an inexcusable oversight. No jealousy need be feared, no animosities can be aroused, by direct praise of Brother Albert H. Zink, past Sovereign Prince of Palmoni Council, Princes of Jerusalem.

Brother Zink has been a hard and effective worker, ever since his introduction to the Scottish Rite bodies, in 1904. His unblemished character, his personal charm, his unselfish thoughtfulness for others, his remakable histrionic talent, his versatility and his energy, have all been contributing factors in stimulating and encouraging interest in the order. His example of loyalty and devotion has served to influence others to emulate his efforts, though with no spirit of rivalry. Lavishly gifted by nature with unusual talent for his work;

possessing a voice of wonderful power, and combining the instincts of the born artist, with intelligent study of his subject, Brother Zink brings to the characterization of the various and varied parts he assumes, a pronounced realism which cannot fail of leaving its impress upon the neophite, no matter how unimpressionable he may be.

Brother Zink's life and activities are so closely interwoven with the interests of the Consistory, that his loss would be almost irreparable. A young man, exemplifying the principles of his Craft in his daily walk and intercourse with his brethren, possessed of health and legitimate ambition, ready at any moment to accept with promptness and energy any task that is presented, he has become a star in the Masonic firmament that canopies the Valley of Buffalo, a star whose brilliancy, it is the hope of the writer, may not be dimmed for many years to come.

His Greatest Role.

In the long list of roles which Brother Zink has from time to time assumed, in none, probably, has he appeared to better advantage than in that of Zerubbabel, the young Hebrew leader who sought and obtained from Darius, the kind-hearted but volatile Babylonish king, permission to return with his brother captives to the city of their fathers, and to rebuild the temple of their God. In this character, the interpretation of Brother Zink has not been excelled. All the inflexible courage, the steadfastness of principle, the devotion to an ideal, the unselfishness and zeal of the ancient, is vividly portrayed. The wonderful appeal to the reason of Darius, the temptation, where personal interests are forgotten in the devotion to a fixed purpose, the fidelity which physical trial cannot quench and the final embellishment of Truth, have given to Brother Zink's work a standard of unapproachable excellence and impressiveness. Nor have his dramatic talents been concealed under the roof of Buffalo Cathedral. His services have been sought and appreciated in other cities, and in other Consistories of the Rite, his intelligent conceptions have won deserved commendation. Even in secular affairs he has become a factor, and the municipal Christmas tree has given added pleasure to the little ones, through his impersonation of the mythical Saint. Thoroughness is a characteristic, as it is the inspiration, of Brother Zink's work. Whether in his Consistory roles, giving a reading before a classical audience, or seeking to amuse in the lighter but no less difficult character of minstrel entertainer, there is always the fixed purpose of giving the very best that is in him, and this fact, added to his ability and versatility have won to this true man and brother, a distinct place among his fellows.

CONSISTORY CHESS CLUB

Takes High Rank as a Popular Organization and Promises Greater Things.

OF the various special organizations which have come into existence within Buffalo Consistory, since the acquisition of the Blocher property and the opening of the beautiful Consistory House, none is more deserving of conspicuous mention than the Consistory Chess Club. Chess is not only a highly scientific, but an ennobling game. The chess enthusiast may be regarded as a thinker and a reasoner. His must be an active and a comprehensive mind. There is no frivolity about chess, and the expert may be set down as a man of clear perceptions, accurate judgment and pronounced intellect. It has been said that the successful chess player would prove a capable general. Probably no game of skill is better calculated to bring into action the higher qualities of the reasoning faculties than this of the ivory knights. The following comprehensive history of the Consistory Chess Club, is furnished us by Dr. Richard S. J. DeNiord, the capable secretary of the Club, who has been a most enthusiastic and efficient officer, as well as a devoted adherent of Consistory ideals. He says:

HISTORY OF BUFFALO CONSISTORY

"The real factors that stand back of any certain event, should be carefully sought and set forth, if a complete history is to be written concerning it. Back of the deed stands the thought. Back of any enterprise is the nucleus responsible for its conception. The birth and the development of any organization can only be in accordance with the amount of vitality in the group of ideas which brings about its conception. These facts ought to be taken into consideration in so far as they should apply to the origin of the Buffalo Consistory Chess Club. Otherwise, there would be very little to say.

"For example, it would be very easy to give the date of organization and the first officers names. But, in view of what has been said, that would not be a history. It would be merely a statement concerning the act of establishing a Chess Club at a given time and place and the names of those elected to office.

"It is not so easy to start at the very beginning. To do so, it is necessary to go back to a time just subsequent to the purchase of the Blocher home—known at the present time as the Consistory House. A group of stalwart chess players had been looking the place over, and holding forth on its great advantages and its many possibilities. They were all impressed with the facilities it would afford to A. A. S. R. bodies that meet in the Orient of Buffalo. As they entered the library—that is now the 1907 room—one of the group, who was busy rolling a cigarette, remarked: 'Say, fellows, wouldn't this be a bully place to play chess?' They all agreed that its location was ideal in every way.

Idea Born To Live.

"The idea was born to live. The next day one of the group presented a set of chess-men to the members of the Consistory interested in the game. But there was no board to play on. That, however, could not stop the idea. An old folding table was pressed into use. Another one of the group procured some paint, and proceeded to mark off a certain number of black squares, until the top of the old table was converted into a chess board. It was then duly inspected by the chess fellows who were present, and they declared that the paint had been well and truly laid on.

"If you love to play the game, you can then imagine how you would feel if you had to await your turn. Imagine, too, trying to play with a bunch of eager advisers all around you. Is it any wonder, under those conditions, that another set of chess men made their appearance and that the top of another folding table was duly and truly decorated with black squares? That helped some, but you couldn't notice it. Every one wanted to get into the game. The chess bug got under several Consistory caps. There was no getting away from it. The only thing to prevent an outbreak of bugitis or chessitis was to confine that bug. But how? At last a way appeared. A club could and would control it. With this object in view, a group of chess fellows met and talked the matter over on Friday, November 27, 1914. It was decided to get in touch with all the other players on the following Friday evening.

"On December 4, 1914, a committee was appointed to take up the matter of forming a Chess Club with the Commander-in-Chief, and report on the next meeting night.

REPORT SUBMITTED.

"At the meeting held on Friday evening, December 11, the committee submitted the following report:

" 'Your committee on arrangements are pleased to announce that the idea of organizing a Chess Club was submitted to the Commander-in-Chief for his approval. He has given his consent to the organization of the Buffalo Consistory Chess Club. He also stated that he would be pleased to assist in every possible way consistant with the Rite, and so long as the Club kept within due bounds. He has also allotted Monday evening to the Club as official Chess Night.' "

"A hearty vote of thanks was given to our Commander-in-Chief for his personal interest in encouragement to the members, and his support of the Club. The first election of the Club was held on Friday evening, December 18, 1914, with the following result:

"Frederick B. Randall, president; Edwin P. Dodge, vice-president; Franklin E. Bard, treasurer; Richard S. J. DeNiord, secretary; Frederick B. Griffith, Jr., chairman of committee on management; George L. Hodgson, chairman on committee

ILL. CHARLES W. MANN, 33°
CUSTODIAN OF BUFFALO CONSISTORY; PAST THRICE POTENT MASTER
OF PALMONI LODGE AND A CAREFUL STUDENT OF
MASONIC HISTORY

of entertainments; Robert I. Mutchler, chairman of press committee.

"At the first regular meeting in 1915, a committee was appointed to draw up a constitution and by-laws. During January and February, progressive chess was played, in order to ascertain the ability of the members to play the game.

Their First Tournament.

"The first tournament began on Monday evening, March 8th, and closed Monday evening, September 22d. Eighteen of the members qualified to enter the lists and a tilt to win either one of the splendid trophies presented by Ill. George K. Staples and Brother Esbon B. Rew. Brother Allan B. Sutcliff won first place, with a percentage of 1,000; Brother Franklin B. Bard won second place with a percentage of 884. In this tournament 578 games, out of a possible 612, were played. Inter-Club Night was held on March 15th. On this occasion the Buffalo Consistory Chess Club was host to the largest gathering of chess fellows ever held in this city. Members from seven different Clubs were present, representing the Y. M. C. A., L. H. S., T. H. S., H. H. S., St. Paul's and Niagara Falls Chess Clubs. Twenty-four tables were in play at the same time during the evening. This tops the highest previous record held by the old Buffalo Chess Club, for sixteen tables in play, and beats all the records in Western New York.

"The Club has played several match games with other local Clubs and return matches with some of them. The second tournament began on October 25, 1915, and will close February 7, 1916. Since the B. C. C. C. entered the field of chess, nearly two thousand individual games have been played by its members. It has entertained and played with Master chess players. It is not ashamed of its record, knowing that there is no disgrace in going down before a more worthy opponent. As a Club, it looks forward unafraid to enter the lists and try a tilt with any other worthy chess fellows.

Now Well Equipped.

"Besides the pleasure which comes from playing the game, the members have also enjoyed the task of overcoming the hundred and one details, that go hand in hand with any progressive organization. Through the kindness of our Commander-in-Chief, our guests have been entertained at his personal expense. Sets of chess-men and chess tables have been provided as the need arose, until the Club's equipment is second to none and fully equal to our present requirements. Under such a propitious condition the Club should grow and flourish.

"And as the Club continues to grow, as it has done from that first set of chess-men, and that first chess table, up to the present time, the stalwarts will not forget the many kindnesses of our big-hearted Commander-in-Chief, nor will they lose sight of the fact that he is constantly striving to foster the weal of every one of the features which he has encouraged to grow up in and about the Consistory House, in an effort to make it the center of all things which are worthy and worth while."

Buffalo Consistory Chess Club has elected officers for 1916, as follows: Edwin P. Dodge, president; Carl W. Knaus, vice-president; Franklin E. Bard, treasurer; Richard S. J. DeNiord, secretary; Esbon R. Rew and Fred B. Randall, directors.

BUFFALO CONSISTORY ENTERTAINERS

An Organization Which Is Doing Its Full Share to Stimulate Interest in Consistory House.

FEW purveyors of amusement have so quickly sprung into deserved popularity as the members of Buffalo Consistory who in the Fall of 1913, under the direction of Brother Harry D. Hosmer, 32°, Secretary of Buffalo Consistory and all the co-ordinate bodies of the Rite in the Valley of Buffalo, banded themselves together to provide varied amusement features, for the more than two thousand members of the Scottish Rite and their friends. Something like 100 of the Brothers, gifted with forensic ability and with a natural taste for the stage and burnt cork, united to make up an organization to be known as "Buffalo Consistory Entertainers." This was done with the approval and consent of Ill. George K. Staples, 33°, Commander-in-Chief, and from the start, demonstrated the capacity of its members to present practically every feature of musical, dramatic and classic stage or drawing-room legitimate entertainment.

From the start, the Consistory Entertainers have been eminently successful, financially and artistically. They have produced more than enough revenue from their various presentations to cover any and all expenses connected with their costuming and equipment. In their first year, they proved such a drawing card, that Rochester Consistory of Rochester, N. Y., on the occasion of their first Ladies' Night, on November 30, 1914, held at the Lyceum Theatre in that city, requested Brother Hosmer's company of artists and funmakers to come to that city and provide the entertainment for their guests. A minstrel entertainment was put on which won the appreciation of an audience that packed the Theatre.

A feature of the organization is that every member, connected with it in any capacity, must be a member of the Buffalo Scottish Rite bodies. This applies equally to performers, orchestra, stage hands, costumers and scenic artists.

Since its organization the Entertainers have five times pleased large audiences at the Consistory, with their complete minstrel program, once at the 74th Armory, once at the Lyric Theatre in Rochester and once at Gowanda, N. Y., under the auspices of Phoenix Lodge, F. & A. M. Added to this, there have been frequent occasions when groups or single individual members, have appeared at private entertainments. An early presentation of a complete new programme is promised by the management in the present year.

Credit to Brother Hosmer.

Success of the Consistory Entertainers has come through good management on the part of Brother Hosmer, by loyal and energetic effort by each individual, in a generous rivalry to excel. There is no lack of talent, no personal jealousies, and the result is a harmonious working organization, that deserves and gains the enthusiastic support of the great fraternal body of which it is a part. The orchestra, drawn from the Entertainers' membership, is under the capable and careful direction of Brother John W. Bolton, 32°, and Brother Ulysses G. Lee, 32°, has full charge of music rehearsals. To these two is due a large measure of the credit for bringing the musical features to their present high plane of excellence.

At the Annual Reunions of Buffalo Consistory, the Entertainers contribute their measure of pleasure to the large number of visitors from other jurisdictions, who have acquired the "habit" of attending these yearly gatherings. It was a happy idea and in its inception brings credit to its originator. It is these varied features of attraction and interest which have served their purpose well, in giving to Buffalo Consistory a just claim upon the attention and approval of the Brethren of sister Consistories, and of the Supreme Council. They reflect not only the ability but the zeal of the Buffalo Brethren, who count not personal sacrifice of time nor effort, in their desire to further the best interests of their beloved Rite.

BUFFALO CONSISTORY BAND

BUFFALO Consistory has reason to be proud of the Band which has been organized from its membership and which has rendered excellent service both for the Consistory and for Ismailia Temple, Nobles of the Mystic Shrine, under the direction of John W. Bolton. It contains an active list of forty-two members; six reserve members; eleven passive members, and seven honorary members; sixty-six in all. "Always ready," is the slogan of this energetic musical organization, no matter what the occasion, for it is from this body of musicians that the Consistory Orchestra is formed, and all wants in the musical line can be supplied on short notice. Following is the active and reserve list, upon which the energetic leader can draw at any time:

Active Members.

Oscar Buchzik, John W. Bolton, J. Adam Bamberg, August F. Bamberg, F. P. Brice, Oscar R. Cott, H. G. Duge, Charles Duge, J. H. Elliott, D. W. Elliott, C. Federlein, Conrad Hoffman, George W. Henseler, John Hirst, J. A. Hulse, Chas. B. Kronenberg, Jay C. King, A. Luebcke, U. G. Lee, Chas. P. Leib, Edwin Murr, C. G. Muskopf, F. L. Muskopf, H. J. Muskopf, Hal

Nelson, D. C. Pierce, W. J. Robinson, Jr., Leopold Roebbig, Fred Seeman, A. E. Saxer, H. G. Sturm, Sr., August Schneider, Carl Tischendorf, C. J. Wannemacher, Adam Weis, A. Weinheimer, Albert A. Williams, Adolph Lorentz, James MacFadyen, Louis W. Petry, Clayton L. Spooner.

Reserve Members.

Rudolph Baumler, Samuel King, Charles G. Moore, Walter L. Ruth, Frank S. Vester, E. M. Waldrip.

ILL. FRANCIS G. WARD, 33°
SUCCESSOR TO ILL. CHARLES W. CUSHMAN AS COMMANDER-IN-CHIEF OF
BUFFALO CONSISTORY, SERVING EFFICIENTLY IN THAT
OFFICE FOR NEARLY A DECADE

ILL. FRANCIS G. WARD, 33°

Second Commander-in-Chief of Buffalo Consistory, Whose Masonic Enthusiasm Strengthened the Local Body.

THOUGH not unexpected, the death of Ill. Francis G. Ward, which occurred on Tuesday, November 16, 1915, was the cause of a great sorrow to the members of Buffalo Consistory and the co-ordinate bodies, in which the former Commander-in-Chief had proven himself a strong developing power. Taking up the duties of presiding officer in the fall of 1903, following the death of Ill. Brother Cushman, he had been chosen Commander-in-Chief at a special election authorized by the Supreme Council on November 27, 1903, and had served the Consistory ably and loyally, from that date, over a period of nearly ten years, until relieved of the responsibility of the office at his own request, at the election of May 24, 1912. At the first meeting following the death of the loved Past Commander, a committee was appointed, composed of Ill. George L. Brown, 33°, Ill. George K. Staples, 33° and Ill. William H. Ellis, 33°, to prepare a suitable memorial to his memory. The following was presented and unanimously adopted:

"IN LOVING MEMORY
OF
ILLUSTRIOUS FRANCIS GRANT WARD, 33°
PAST COMMANDER-IN-CHIEF
OF
BUFFALO CONSISTORY
ANCIENT ACCEPTED SCOTTISH RITE
FOR THE NORTHERN MASONIC
JURISDICTION OF THE
UNITED STATES OF AMERICA

Whose earthly light was extinguished

on

Tuesday, November 16, 1915.

"For fifteen consecutive years in public office, by the suffrage of his fellow citizens, his career was an expression of unwearied zeal, energy and devotion, which was an inspiration to those within the zone of his influence and which left a deep impression upon the civic life of this municipality. His breadth of vision foresaw the City's need, and the execution of the responsibilities entrusted to him, found fulfillment in ample and generous measure.

"A lover of his country, he sprang to the defense of its flag when duty called and attained the rank of Colonel.

"He had learned his Masonic lessons well, and he wielded the sword of his intellect, influence and power, always in the spirit of charity, and forbearance. His hand was always outstretched to aid the fallen and the distressed. His tongue was ever ready to speak the words of encouragement to those whose mental burdens seemed heavy. Beneath a brusque and rough exterior there was the heart of a child—tender and sympathetic and helpful to his fellowmen.

"In the home a loving father; in public life a man of resource as well as execution—a builder up of civic greatness; among his friends a loyal companion with a buoyant and congenial spirit, overflowing with good-fellowship.

"He did his best, he played the man,
His way was straight, his soul was clean;
His failings not unkind, nor mean,
He loved, he helped his fellowman.

"His memory will be cherished in our hearts throughout our earthly journey. We place this simple tribute of our love and esteem in the records of the Consistory as a testimonial of our affection for him.

> GEORGE L. BROWN,
> GEORGE K. STAPLES,
> WILLIAM H. ELLIS."

To the members of Buffalo Consistory, the life and work of Ill. Francis G. Ward are a striking example, of the accomplishments which come from a proper assimilation of brains, energy and determination, in the composition of the average American youth. In both his public and Masonic life, he has set a worthy example, and his memory is enshrined in the love of a multitude of hearts among his brethren and outside that broad circle.

Francis G. Ward was born near Jordan, Cayuga County, N. Y., in 1856. His birthplace was on a farm, the Ward homestead being upon a grant made to Col. John Ward, Francis's great-grandfather, for services in the Revolutionary War. The Wards were a race of patriots, and it is not surprising that the Consistory's late Commander-in-Chief was imbued with the same spirit. Col. Thomas Ward, Francis's grandfather, went to Texas in 1836 and served under General Sam. Houston. He died in Huntsville, Texas, after the annexation of that territory to the United States. Major Herman G. Ward, the father of Francis, also served in Texas with his father, later returning to the North and holding the position of quartermaster during the Civil War. In 1864 he became one of the principal owners of the American Express Company.

Young Ward's education was not neglected, in fact every advantage was afforded to fit him for his natural choice of a profession, that of civil engineer. In 1864 he was sent to the Rectory School at Hamden, Ct. From thence in 1866 he was taken to Paris and placed in the Institution Cousin-Lycee Bonaparte until the Franco-Prussian War in 1870. He then returned to Hamden for a year, but in 1871 went to France and entered the College Chaptal, where he remained until 1873. In 1875 he returned to New York and entered the service of the Laflin & Rand Powder Company. He was sent to Buffalo to take charge of the Buffalo branch of the company in the same year.

In 1877 young Ward entered the employ of the New York Central & Hudson River Railroad, in New York City. He held successively the position of yardmaster, dispatcher, station master and assistant to the general manager at the Grand Central station, until December, 1885, when he was appointed General Superintendent and Engineer of the Panama Railroad, on the Isthmus of Panama. While in that position he fully proved his ability as an engineer and his capacity for work. He reconstructed the wharves, railroad bridges and plants destroyed during the revolution of 1885, as well as two larger bridges, in 1887, for the Canal Company, crossing the Chiqus river and costing $800,000. He was transferred to the Paris office of the Canal Company as chargi of railroad affairs, in 1887. In 1888 he entered the service of the Societe de Travaux Publics of Paris, as a member of the Technical Structural Commission, in charge of the construction of the Turkish Asiatic railroads. He had charge of the bridge location and construction for the road until 1890, when he resigned to return to Buffalo to take charge of the affairs of the R. W. Bell Manufacturing Company, which he conducted until 1896, when the Company retired from business.

In Public Life.

On May 15, 1896, he was appointed Superintendent of Water, by the Commissioners of Public Works, serving until 1898, when he was appointed

Lieutenant Colonel of the 202d New York, United States Volunteers, by Governor Black. He served during the Cuban War, with credit, retaining his command until the regiment was mustered out in 1899. He was elected Commissioner of Public Works of the City of Buffalo in 1901, and was re-elected in 1903 and 1907, serving until the time of his death. In the primaries of October last, the wonderful hold which the Commissioner of Public Works retained upon the public, was well displayed in the first election to designate nominations under the new form of Commission government, when he ran far ahead of all contestants in a field of forty-six ambitious aspirants. That he was not re-elected at the subsequent election in November, was due entirely to the fact that it was well-known that his health would not permit his performance of the duties of the office, if elected. His candidacy was not of his own seeking, but an expression of the unchanging loyalty and devotion of friends.

His Record as a Mason.

Ill. Francis G. Ward was indeed a "square stone in the Temple of Masonry." On his return to Buffalo from Europe in 1890 he soon became a member of Ancient Landmarks Lodge, No. 441, F. & A. M., and served as a Master of that Lodge in 1896. On November 28, 1901, his petition for membership was presented to Palmoni Lodge of Perfection, and he received the 14th degree, Grand Elect Mason on February 25, 1902. He became a member of Rochester Consistory in the same year and in 1903, was appointed Second Lieutenant-Commander of Buffalo Consistory, under dispensation. His advancement to Commander-in-Chief has been fully detailed. In all his Masonic work, Ill. Brother Ward displayed the same energy, loyalty and determination as had characterized his civic career. Under his leadership, following the demise of Ill. Brother Cushman, the Scottish Rite continued to flourish in the Valley of Buffalo even more vigorously. As a presiding officer he was firm but never dictatorial; his decisions were prompt, his reasoning incisive.

As a degree worker, he gave to his characters an impressive personality which could not fail of its effect upon the candidate. His sturdy figure, his heavy voice, his compelling manner, made him a born leader of men, and yet his natural power of influence was never applied in an arbitrary or unreasonable manner. He gained the esteem and regard of his co-workers, by the force of example, as well as by the magnetism of his personality. His last rendition of the part of Frederick in the Twentieth, his favorite degree, will long retain a place in the memory of those brothers who were so fortunate as to be present, on that occasion. The writer can only express approval and appreciation of the words of the Illustrious Brothers who framed his memorial. His light is extinguished; the working tools of life have been laid away, but his influence and his inspirations hang like sweet incense about the Cathedral, where he wrought so long and so well, a lasting perfume that time cannot dissipate.

ILL. SAMUEL ROOT, 33°

Treasurer of Palmoni Lodge for Twenty-six Years and Later of All Co-ordinate Bodies.

OF the older members of Buffalo Consistory and its co-ordinate Bodies, none are more deserving of special mention and approval for loyalty and faithful service, than Ill. Samuel Root, who for twenty-six years has handled the funds of Lodge, Council, Chapter and Consistory, in a manner to disarm criticism and inspire implicit faith. Following his induction into the Ineffable grades of Palmoni Lodge, in 1882, immediately after the reorganization of the Lodge subsequent to the big fire, he became active, serving in various subordinate positions until 1889, when he was appointed and elected treasurer of Palmoni Lodge and Palmoni Council. Later, on the organization of Buffalo Chapter of Rose Croix and Buffalo Consistory, he was appointed to a similar position in both those bodies, and has served in this four-headed office ever since.

While not a demonstrative member of the Craft, Illustrious Brother Root has been a tower of strength to the Buffalo Bodies. His loyalty has stimulated others; his wise counsel has been sought and followed by Commanders and Thrice Potent Masters; his daily life has been an example

ILL. SAMUEL ROOT, 33°
FOR TWENTY-SIX YEARS TREASURER OF PALMONI LODGE AND PALMONI
COUNCIL, AND OF CHAPTER AND CONSISTORY
SINCE THEIR ORGANIZATION

of practical Masonry. In the golden autumn of his days his bark floats on an untroubled sea. He has well earned the Masonic honors which have come to him. To receive the crown of a Sovereign Grand Inspector General at the hands of the Supreme Council, and from his Buffalo brethren the distinction of being made a life member of the four Scottish Rite Bodies, was no more than the just expression of approval for meritorious service in the interests of the Rite. It is the wish of his Brethren that he may long live to enjoy the satisfying reflections of duty well performed.

MASONIC CONNECTIONS.

Samuel Root was born October 7, 1837, at Lubec, Washington County, Maine, a direct descendant of John Root, in the seventh generation, who emigrated from the town of Badby, England, and settled in the town of Farmington, Conn., in 1640, one of the original settlers. Samuel was educated in the village school and at Washington Academy, East Machias, Me., completing his education in 1853.

He removed from Lubec, Me., to Fall River, Mass., in 1859, and to Buffalo in 1870. Symbolic Degrees: He was initiated Entered Apprentice, Dec. 16, 1857; passed to degree of Fellowcraft, Dec. 23, 1857, and raised to the Sublime Degree of Master Mason, Feb. 5, 1858, in Washington Lodge No. 37, at Lubec, Me. He was made a Chapter Mason in Fall River, Mass., in a Chapter under dispensation, receiving the Mark Master degree on Nov. 21, 1864; Past Master, the same evening; Excellent Master, Nov. 29, 1864, and Royal Arch, Nov. 29, 1864.

He was not made a Royal and Select Master until March 10, 1881, in Buffalo Council, No. 17, although becoming a Knight Templer, Oct. 4, 1866, in Sutton Commandery, No. 16, New Bedford, Mass. He received the Ineffable grades of the Scottish Rite on March 3, 1882 in Palmoni Lodge of Perfection; Historical and Traditional grades March 3, 1882, in Palmoni Council, Princes of Jerusalem; the Philosophical and Doctrinal grades March 10, 1884, in Rochester Chapter of Rose Croix, and the Philosophical and Chivalric grades, March 20, 1884, in Rochester Consistory. He was created and crowned a Sovereign Grand Inspector General in Boston, Mass., September 18, 1900. Brother Root demitted from Rochester Consistory in 1893 and was one of the original charter members of Buffalo Consistory. He was appointed and elected Treasurer of Palmoni Lodge, and Council, April 26, 1889; appointed and elected Treasurer of Buffalo Consistory, Sept. 21, 1893. He holds a life membership in Buffalo Chapter and Lake Erie Commandery, as well as the Scottish Rite Bodies.

CONSISTORY SAXOPHONE CHOIR

ON January 4, 1915, was organized the Consistory Saxophone Choir. In its membership is included five worthy brothers who are musical enthusiasts, as well as capable performers. They are: Brothers David W. Elliott, soprano; Charles G. Moore, alto; Morris A. Banks, tenor; Frank S. Vester, tenor; Carl W. Knaus, baritone. Every Sunday morning, an hour previous to the time set for the Consistory Band rehearsal, the members of this excellent choir get together in the large hall on the second floor of the Cathedral, and with the portraits of Buffalo's growing galaxy of Illustrious 33ds, looking down upon them with approval, practice the most popular classic music, with which they are well supplied. Their repertoir is extensive and selected with excellent judgment. Afterward they take their regular places in the Band rehearsal. The Saxophone Choir has rendered valuable and commendable service in certain of the Consistory work, a combination of the saxophones with five clarinets and two flutes, giving admirable effect in the 24th degree. To the choir director, Brother Carl W. Knaus, must be given credit, for having added so attractive and desirable an organization to the Consistory's extended list of entertaining features.

ILL. CHARLES W. MANN, 33°

FOR ten years Ill. Charles W. Mann, 33°, Past Thrice Potent Master of Palmoni Lodge, has been custodian of the Consistory, in which he received the 32° in the class of 1904, at the first reunion. Brother Mann's Masonic record is more extensive than falls to the lot of most of his brethren. In both the Scottish and York Rites he has been active, filling numerous positions of responsibility and honor. Brother Mann was initiated in King Solomon's Lodge No. 91, F. & A. M., on January 20, 1881, and was raised to the Sublime Degree of Master Mason on February 24, 1881, at Troy, N. Y. Immediately after becoming a member of Palmoni Lodge and Buffalo Consistory in 1904, Brother Mann entered upon an active career as a worker in the various degrees, and today holds the enviable record of having worked in every degree, from the 4th to the 32d inclusive, in some capacity, usually holding an important position, frequently acting as the presiding officer of the degree.

He was elected Thrice Potent Master of Palmoni Lodge in 1905 and gave commendable service. In the York Rite, Brother Mann's activity in the earlier days of his Masonic career was earnest and faithful. He was exalted to the Sub-

ANCIENT ACCEPTED SCOTTISH RITE

lime Degree of Royal Arch Mason in 1881, and was elected and served as High Priest of Apollo Chapter, No. 48, 1887, 1888 and 1889. He received the Templar degrees in Apollo Commandery in 1883, and demitted to Lake Erie Commandery, in 1898, holding the office of Prelate in that body from 1901 to 1904, inclusive. In military and civic affairs Brother Mann has been actively interested.

OF AMERICAN STOCK.

Ill. Brother Mann was born in Glenn's Falls, N. Y., September 11, 1853, coming of good American stock, being a grandson of Moody Mann, a nephew of T. Mann, whose grave is marked by a small stone on Breed's Hill, Boston, where the real battle, erroneously called Bunker Hill, was fought. Patriotic ardor is a distinguishing trait of Ill. Brother Mann, love of the Craft and love of country, being synonymous, with the efficient custodian of the Consistory. It was he who was largely responsible for the famous Consistory flags. He has been an earnest and careful student of Masonic history, and probably no man in Buffalo possesses a wider knowledge of Symbolic, Capitular, Cryptic or Chivalric Masonry than he. This knowledge particularly fits him for the responsible position he occupies in the Consistory and Co-ordinate bodies, where appropriate costuming and stage arrangement are eminently essential for the proper presentation of the numerous degrees. He is a thorough ritualist, and his pen has not been idle in the dissemination of Masonic light and knowledge, to his less informed brethren.

IN MEMORIAM

To those who wrought in earlier days
   To lay foundation broad and strong;
Who led our halting steps away
   From all the snares of Pagan wrong,
Who blazed the way, in noble course
   For us to follow down the years,
Our thoughts oft turn in fond regret,
   Our eyes bedewed with silent tears.

They builded well, they builded sure,
   They drew designs both strong and bold
Upon the Trestle Board, for us
   As workmen faithful, to uphold;
As those who, coming later, sought
   To follow well the guiding light,
So we shall strive, until the end,
   To stronger build our sacred Rite.

Not Prince, or Potentate on any throne,
   Not Knight or Peasant in their train,
Ruled more with love and equity,
   Or nobler deeds could well attain.
We honor those who bravely wrought
   In apron white, or purple gown
Until they, at Divine command,
   The Working Tools of Life laid down.

                                        J. L. N.

EARLY MASONIC LODGE

IT is a matter of interest to Masons everywhere, that the oldest Lodge of Masons anywhere in the country west of the Alleghany Mountains, is in Marietta, O. This Lodge was constituted at Waterman's Tavern, Roxbury, Mass., February 20, 1776. It had a traveling charter and worked in the patriot army until April 23, 1783. George Washington and others prominent in the American Revolution, have attended communications of this Lodge. The pioneers of the Northwest Territory brought the charter with them to Marietta, where the Lodge began work June 28, 1790, that being the first time as far as is known, that a Masonic Lodge held a communication west of the Alleghany Mountains. The seal of this Lodge consists of thirteen links united, forming a circle enclosing two clasped hands. Those constituting the Lodge, believed that the thirteen English colonies, would become independent and unite together as States. They put their faith into the seal of the Lodge. This seal was designed by Benjamin Franklin and was engraved by Paul Revere, according to Rev. E. A. Coil.

ILL. JOHN L. BROTHERS, 33°

For Many Years Active in Masonic Work, Holding Responsible Offices in Both the York and Scottish Rites.

SINCE the foregoing pages were written, the Grim Messenger has inflicted serious loss in Masonic circles, by the removal of Ill. John L. Brothers from the scene of life's activities. In the ripeness of years, our beloved Brother was summoned on February 22, while on a visit to his daughter, Mrs. James J. Bailey, at Englewood Park, N. J. The body of our Illustrious Brother was brought to Buffalo and laid to rest in Forest Lawn, after the impressive services of the Knights Templar and of the 33d degree had been observed in Buffalo Consistory. In paying final tribute to one who had given liberally of his time and energy to advance the interests of his beloved Rite, the brethren of the York and Scottish Rites, gave full expression of their sorrow at the great loss sustained, and demonstrated the high esteem and honor in which their former associate was held by the members of the Craft, as a Man and Mason.

John L. Brothers was initiated in Queen City Lodge, No. 358, F. & A. M., in 1865, being raised to the Sublime Degree of Master Mason, on April 2d. He served as Junior and Senior Warden of

ILL. JOHN L. BROTHERS, 33°
PRESIDING OFFICER FOR MANY YEARS OF THE CHAPTER OF
ROSE CROIX. A FAMOUS RITUALIST

that Lodge and was elected Master, but declined to accept that responsible office. He was exalted to the rank of Royal Arch Mason, on June 18, 1870, in Keystone Chapter, 163, and served as Excellent High Priest, during 1881-2. He was made a Royal and Select Master, in Keystone Council, No. 20, June 18, 1870, and held the office of Thrice Illustrious Master of that body, in 1877-8-80-3-4. He was created a Knight Templar, in Hugh dePayens Commandery, March 14, 1871, and was its Commander in 1881 and again in 1885. He was honored by being elected Grand Master of the Grand Council R. & S. M., of the State of New York, in 1888.

In the Scottish Rite, the energetic brother soon gained distinction. His petition was presented in Palmoni Lodge of Perfection April 2, 1889, and the degrees of the Lodge and of Palmoni Council were conferred upon him on that date. He was made a member of Rochester Chapter of Rose Croix, April 4, 1889, and received the 32d degree in Rochester Consistory on the same evening. Illustrious Brother Brothers was one of the first members of Buffalo Consistory to become an honorary member of the Supreme Council, Sovereign Grand Inspectors-General, of the 33d and Last Degree of the Ancient Accepted Scottish Rite.

These honors were well deserved, for no member of Buffalo Consistory ever worked more earnestly or effectively to bring the ceremonies of the

Rite to the highest perfection. As the first Most Wise Master of Buffalo Chapter of Rose Croix, he instilled into that body an ambition for thoroughness and ritualistic correctness, which has had its influence upon his successors. Although not an officer in the other bodies of the Rite, his interest was active and helpful.

Ill. John L. Brothers was born in Albany, on March 24, 1835. He came with his parents to Buffalo in 1849, at the age of fourteen, and remained a resident of this city until his death. He was active in civic affairs, and from 1900 to 1909, inclusive, was Superintendent of Parks.

The impressive funeral services held at Buffalo Consistory Cathedral were under the direction of Commander Thomas S. Watts of Hugh De Payens Commandery No. 30, Knights Templar, assisted by Eminent Sir Charles S. Butler as Prelate. Following this ceremony there was a brief ceremony in which the 33d degree Masons participated under the leadership of Illustrious George K. Staples, Commander-in-Chief of the Buffalo Consistory, and Illustrious Jerome L. Cheney of Syracuse, acting as Deputy for the Scottish Rite Masons of the State of New York.

The Grand Commandery of Knights Templar was represented by Right Eminent William E. Elmendorf, Grand Commander.

The Grand Council of the State over which Ill. Brothers presided as Grand Master in 1887 was represented by Most Illustrious William H. Ellis, Grand Master, Most Illustrious Abraham Oppenheimer and Most Illustrious Fred E. Ogden, Past Grand Masters, and Right Illustrious William S. Riselay, Grand Representative of the Grand Council of New Hampshire, and Right Illustrious Edgar C. Neal, Grand Representative of the Grand Council of South Carolina. The General Grand Council of the United States was represented by M. P. George A. Newell, of Medina, N. Y., General Grand Master.

The active bearers were Sir Knights George Reimann, Charles A. Smith, Alvin W. Day, Roswell M. Norton, Burt P. Hoyer, Alvin L. Higley, Louis H. Knapp, James B. Snelgrove. The honorary bearers were Past Commanders of Hugh de Payens Commandery, Sir Knights William F. Elmendorf, William H. Lyons, John H. Hull, J. William Prouse, Charles S. Butler, William S. Riselay, Millington Lockwood, Martin H. Blecher, Clark H. Hammond; and 33d Degree Masons as follows:

George E. Clarke, George Clinton, Francis T. Coppins, William H. Ellis, Walter D. Greene, Harry L. Taylor, Herbert P. Bissell, Walter M. Gibson, Robert C. Titus, Alan H. G. Hardwicke, Charles E. Hayes, Howard D. Herr, Joseph H. Horton, Frank B. Hower, Charles W. Mann, Joel H. Prescott, Samuel Root, George K. Staples and Otto W. Volger.

Buffalo Chapter of Rose Croix was represented in the final ceremonies by Most Wise Master, Charles Elbert Rhodes, and Palmoni Council

Princes of Jerusalem, by Sovereign Prince, James L. Nixon.

Buffalo Consistory has much for which to thank the early loyalty and devotion of those energetic Brothers who have answered the summons of the Grand Architect. To Cushman, Fellows, Ward, Markham, Noble, Wadsworth and Benson must ever go a large measure of credit for the remarkable progress which the Scottish Rite has made in the Orient of Buffalo; and clear down the years, their memory will be treasured, and their example will be an incentive to continued loyalty on the part of their survivors and successors.

www.ingramcontent.com/pod-product-compliance
Lightning Source LLC
Chambersburg PA
CBHW061633040426
42446CB00010B/1393